The
Catalog of
Lost Books

For Judith Ann Schiff—
with fond memories of
the Rare Book Room—

Tod Vulgn

March 1994

Also by Tad Tuleja

NONFICTION: Fabulous Fallacies
Namesakes
Curious Customs
The Cat's Pajamas
The Riddle of Cheiron
Foreignisms

FICTION: The Kak-Abdullah Conspiracy
Mark of the Vulture
The Devil's Triangle
Land of Precious Snow

The Catalog of Lost Books

An Annotated and Seriously Addled Collection of Great Books that Should Have Been Written But Never Were

TAD TULEJA

FAWCETT COLUMBINE · NEW YORK

For
the Ridgewalker
from
Alec

La verdad, cuya madre es la historia,
émula del tiempo, depósito de las acciones,
testigo de lo pasado, ejemplo y aviso de
lo presente, advertencia de lo por venir.

—*Pierre Menard*

Ein Humbug für Alle und Keinen.

—*Alexander Yarrowville*

Contents

Introduction

"A la Recherche des Tomes Perdus"

Not quite eighty years ago, in an oak and leather study in darkest Boston, the president of Harvard University, Charles William Eliot, remarked casually to a friend, "One could get a first-class education from a shelf of books five feet long."

That comment—so succinctly magisterial, so tantalizing in its promise of instant learning—inspired a collection of "great books" known officially as the Harvard Classics and unofficially as "Dr. Eliot's Five-Foot Shelf." In fifty volumes and some 22,000 pages, it embraced the entire range of those writings—from Homer to Tennyson, from Confucius to John Stuart Mill—thought worthy of attention at the time. The focus of this mammoth undertaking, in the modest summation of general editor Eliot, was "serious reading of the highest quality." Its purpose was to "present so ample and characteristic a record of the stream of the world's thought that the observant reader's mind shall be enriched, refined, and fertilized by it."

The collection was an instant and enduring hit. Between its initial publication in 1910 and the appearance of Robert Maynard Hutchins's Great Books of the Western World forty years later, the Harvard Classics practically defined liberal education. One who had read these fifty volumes, or at least could drop their authors' names at appropriate moments, was considered ipso facto "well rounded." Every library in the land owned a set. Upwardly mobile families displayed their sets as prominently as their descendants display first folios. Right-thinking teachers forged their own "great books" lists by raiding Dr. Eliot's table of contents—and they are still doing so today.

But there's a catch. As respectful as I am of Eliot's achievement, and as loath as I am to attack our educational Lourdes, honesty compels me to point out that the good doctor's editorial philosophy betrayed a certain (how shall I say it?) Brahminic, Cantabrigian provinciality. There is an entire dimension to "great writing"—I would call it the dimension of "radical whimsy"—to which the Harvard professor was oblivious.

I first became aware of this dimension through the fortuitous entry into my life of Myra Quinn.

It was about a year and a half ago, at a cocktail party somewhere north of Zabar's. You know the type. One of those bottled-water-and-goose-liver affairs where caustic remarks about the decline of Cancún jockey for position with Diderot anecdotes and the latest word on the Serbo-Croatian novel. I was knocking off my third Tequila Sunrise when a fragment of Eliot-inspired chitchat wafted over my shoulder like an intrusive melody—the fast-food jingle you just can't stop humming.

First, a reedy voice, like an oboe submerged in sauterne, began a too-familiar refrain:

"Ontologically speaking, Pantagruel is bodied forth with less amplitude of vision than any other character in the picaresque tradition."

Then the response, like a clarinet needing cork work:

"*Bien sûr*, but in terms of sheer facticity, don't you agree that the Rabelaisian oeuvre is still the acme of the genre?"

Like everyone else with a liberal education, I had heard such conversations before; indeed, they had shadowed my entire adult life. And I had learned to parry them as well as anyone I knew, usually with nothing more combative than a stifled yawn. I don't know what was different about this night, but I found myself suddenly peeved beyond rescue, and I turned in the reedy duo's direction.

They looked agreeable enough. Topsiders, patched elbows, thinning hair. Gesturing at each other with Perrier bottles. Although I had never met them before, I felt an instant, biting sense of camaraderie: somewhere on their bodies, I was certain, they bore the Muses' secret sign, the tweed birthmark.

"If you chaps want the acme of the picaresque," I suddenly

heard myself saying, "surely you're tilling the wrong field. The genre didn't peak until 1845. Myra Quinn's *Six Years with a Donkey*. Magisterial."

It stopped them cold. Obviously they had never heard of Myra Quinn—how could they? I had just made her up—and they had not a clue how to respond. Their eyes flickered shock and indecision. Should they call me on the gambit, or remain silent? Demand details about the interloper, risking a supercilious "Gotcha"? Or play along, hoping I wouldn't press *them* for details? It was, as Aristotle might have put it, a sweet moment.

Discretion being the better part of banter, I removed myself from the premises quickly after this *touché*, escorting Myra on the arm of my imagination. My subsequent stroll to the subway proved smugly, and thus richly, satisfying, and it got me to thinking more about Myra. Idly at first, and then propelled, I suppose, by the same lust for pattern that keeps Will Wang in business, I began to concoct details for my hoax. What I came up with first was this sketch:

> Myra Quinn, the last of fourteen children born to Harry Quinn, a Philadelphia eggbeater designer, and his wife Alma (known as the Mushroom Queen of the Alleghenies), left home in 1829 for "parts south," soon hooked up with a Cherokee guide known as "Donkey," and spent the next six years with him, wandering the hills. Her account of their journey through Jacksonian America, published as Six Years with a Donkey, *has been described as "*Don Quixote *without the quibbling."*

By the time I reached my hovel that evening, I was beginning to hear Myra's voice clearly, and my pockets bulged with napkins full of notes. Then, my appetite whetted and my lunatic fires still raging, I turned to what I saw as Myra's Friends—other creatures from the black lagoon of imagined history who might serve to deflate a pedant or charm a friend. Sometime between midnight and dawn, I had added to my growing writers' stable these additional Mighty Scribblers Who Never Were:

* Eskaduin, the Basque poet whose *Gascon Chronicle* (see page 25) denounces Charlemagne's nephew Roland as a "lapdog" and the Frankish emperor himself as the "Pig King";
* Jeremy Ludlow, author of *Pair of Dice Lost* (page 70), in which God and Satan gamble for control of Creation;
* Lucien Choufleur, whose Sartrean private dick *Raymond Salaud* (page 161) makes Dirty Harry look like Mary Poppins;
* And of course the paragon of undervalued authors, Anonymous, who gave us, among other masterpieces, the *Rotenaksaga*, *Dinarzade's Revenge*, and *The Flute Thief* (pages 27, 43, and 61).

After several such errant adventures in the domain of false-prophet creation, and with my combative mood considerably lightened, I began to suspect I might be onto something. Perhaps I was not the only person in Gotham—or, dare I say it, the Western World—weary of Intelligent Conversation, hungering without wanting to admit it for pins to prick pedants' balloons. Surely there were others out there—sporting their own patched elbows, quaffing their own Tequila Sunrises—who would enjoy meeting Myra and her friends.

That passing fancy was the seed of this catalog. It includes winking brief discussions of one hundred classics that *should* have been written but never were. Partly pseudobiographical, part pseudo-historical, and thoroughly ridiculous, it is designed both as a corrective to Great Books cocktail chatter and as an affectionate swipe at Deep Thinking.

Don't get me wrong. My intention is to complement, not replace. I like Homer as well as the next guy. But what about long forgotten Toto (page 8), the Balkan poet who wrote the "real" *Iliad*? Sure, Joyce is a master of stream of consciousness. But what about neglected Mimsy Borogrove (page 163), who gave us a five-hundred-page novel in one sentence?

To assess whether *The Catalog of Lost Books* should stand beside Dr. Eliot's brainchild on your bookshelf, I suggest you ask yourself a few questions. You're au courant. You subscribe to a little magazine. The name García Márquez rings a bell. But (be honest, now) do you really look forward with any sentiment but dread to your next tête-à-tête on postmodern architecture? Don't the words "semiotics" and "phenomenology" make you reach for a Tums? Don't you sometimes wish you had never learned to tell Anaïs Nin, Djuna Barnes, and Isak Dinesen apart?

Most important of all, wouldn't your life be a whole lot more fun if, the next time some Perrier-sipping tweedo started analyzing the marginalia of Otto Rank, you could whammy him with an even more obscure shrink?

If you can answer yes—even a tentative, nervous yes—to these questions, you should give this catalog a fair test.

Take Otto Rank, for example. If you will turn to the discussion of Bernard Fresh (page 144), you will find more than enough ersatz data from his tome *The Metab Factor* to deflate not only Rank enthusiasts, but psychobabblers of any persuasion.

Or suppose you are cornered by a Wittgensteinian. By my rough estimate there are now 2.3 Wittgensteinians at every literary gathering in the world. They have become the Nietzschean pests of our time, and they cannot be dispersed by straightforward argument. What you need to extricate yourself from the clutches of a Wittgensteinian is a nonchalant reference to Bubba Wilson. In Wilson's slim tractatus *How to Think Good* (page 174), you will find Ludwig's Big Mistake skewered deftly—in fifty words that fit any occasion.

It is possible, of course, that not everyone will be thoroughly enchanted by a catalog of books that never were. If you like your belles lettres straight, if you suspect that spoofs of this sort create "confusion," if you think that Borges should have stuck to card-cataloging, then take this notice as fair warning: you will definitely feel more "secure" with the Great Books that everybody already knows.

But if you've got a spirit of adventure, if you think that Truth can withstand a little ribbing, if you like your conversations, like your drinks, with a grain of salt—then *The Catalog of Lost Books* deserves your serious (not too serious) consideration.

This catalog does not, as Dr. Eliot's compendium was intended to do, present anything so "ample and characteristic" as a "record of the stream of the world's thought." It does not pretend to be a rose. I offer it instead as a wild mushroom: proudly lowborn, vigorous, and possibly dangerous. Not as pretty, or as predictable, as the rosy classics, *The Catalog of Lost Books* is a sporting volume. It's 3.94 times more honest than postmodern architecture. And, I trust, a good deal more fun.

I like to think that Rabelais would approve. I know for sure that Myra Quinn does.

T.T.
Cold Springs

The
Catalog of
Lost Books

The Altamira Spiral (ca. 15,000 B.C.)

"The Master of Magdalene"

The oldest known "book" in the world is not a book as we know it, but an arrangement of polished, inscribed stones from the Altamira cave in northern Spain. Like the cave's more famous bison murals, the stones were discovered in 1879 by spelunker Marcelino de Sautuola; and like the murals, they were immediately dismissed as forgeries, clearly beyond the skill of Paleolithic peoples. Radiocarbon dating has since verified the antiquity of the paintings, but not so that of the inscriptions. The stones themselves are clearly Magdalenian (15,000–10,000 B.C.), but there is no infallible method for determining whether a Cro-Magnon cave dweller or a modern Spaniard (de Sautuola, for example) made the markings. The field of paleoliterature is still riven by controversy over the age of this fascinating scratched "text."

It may legitimately be described as a text because, unlike other Stone Age petroglyphs, the Altamira stones tell a story. When Sautuola found them, he said, they were arranged on the cave floor in a spiral pattern. Following the line of the stones from the "loose end" into the center, he found that the glyphs were grouped repeatedly in "syntactical" structures, and that when subjected to code analysis, the markings yielded a "narrative line." "This spiral," he wrote in 1881, "is the personal testament of a Magdalenian master whom we may accurately call the world's first writer. And the story he tells is a terrible one: it speaks of invention and magic and fear and banishment and death."

More specifically, what Sautuola got from the stones was the tale of a man and a woman who discover that they can communicate with strangers by the use of pictures scratched into pebbles, expressing the concept "bison," for example, by the elementary pictograph or the idea of friendship by the depiction of an open hand, thus: Using such pictures, they create a primitive "dictionary" (Sautuola called it a "petrographary") which they use to communicate outside of their clan. This angers their clan leaders, who, jealous of their popularity, condemn the use of the stones and wall the couple up inside a cave. In that cave, he concludes, they produce their spiral legacy before they die.

The extravagance of Sautuola's conclusions, based as they were on ambiguous scratchings, made him the object of academic scorn, but recent scholarship has tended to vindicate him. Wilma Pedernal y Piedra of the University of Santander, using computer-assisted semiotic resolution techniques, has shown that her nineteenth-century countryman had the narrative basically right, in spite of his bent for grandiosity. "When he calls the pair the planet's first peacemakers, Sautuola goes out on a limb. But of their primacy as writers, not to mention artists 'suicided by society,' there can no longer be any doubt."

Pedernal's confidence, it should be admitted, is not shared by all paleocritics. To many, accepting petrography as writing is carrying respect for the primitive to ludicrous extremes; and even those who accept the inclusion are divided on the meaning of the Altamira "text." French protolinguist Raoul Lascaux, for example, has denounced the Sautuola version as an "irreparably stoned translation, absolutely insensitive to the nuances of Paleolithic grammar." For his full analysis, and Pedernal's response, see the symposium *Glyphanalysis: Recent Fieldwork* (1982), masterfully edited by Venus Willendorf. For Sautuola's readings of representative pebbles, see Appendix A of this volume.

Inventories of Knossos *(ca. 1450 B.C.)*

The Cretan Eraser

One of the archaeological coups of modern times was Michael Ventris's 1952 decoding of the Mycenaean script known as Linear B. By demonstrating that this hitherto indecipherable syllabary was an archaic form of Greek, the young Englishman delighted Hellenists who had wanted proof that Homer's "Achaeans" spoke "Athenian." And by showing that the Linear B tablets found at Knossos were largely inventories of royal possessions, he confirmed the stereotype of Mycenae's "Golden Age" as an era of unsurpassed affluence. But there were also disappointments, for the key to this mysterious period of antiquity seemed to unlock only a room full of goods—almost nothing was heard of kings or religion or "events." In the frustrated words of classicist Marios Phillipides, "It's quite exasperating to know the weight of the royal cows, and not the name of the ruler."

If Babylonist Hans F. G. Utterbock is correct, however, we shall soon have not only the ruler's name, but a Mesopotamian-inspired cosmology, which, Ventris and his colleagues failed to see, was embedded in the inventories all the time. Utterbock, of course, is best known for proving that the cuneiform "inventories" of ancient Babylon contain, in code, the laws of Hammurabi and the Gilgamesh epic. Turning his graphological lights on Linear B, he has discovered that a single scribe, whom he calls the Cretan Eraser, obviously "doctored" over half of Knossos's two thousand tablets, producing a double-layered text that functions not only as chattel listing but also as "the blood song of creation."

His primary evidence for this assertion—published in the notorious 1983 monograph *Sacred Cows and Bull Pizzles: New Light on Linear B*—comes from the prominence of cattle in the Knossos listings. All the scribes mention cows, but in the Eraser's redactions, each heifer is identified by an "omphalos number." Utterbock finds this "anything but surprising." Relating the scribe's "bovine thread" to the contemporaneous "thread of Ariadne," he shows that both the Knossos inventories and the myth of the labyrinth's Minotaur evolved from Middle Eastern bull cults—and even more wondrously, that the sequence of the Eraser's omphalos numbers provides a mathematical model for Daedalus's floor plan. "The structural similarity is unmistakable," he writes. "The Cretans, no less than the Babylonians, explained the cosmos as the rough mating of bull and heifer. Whether through personal genius or royal command, the Cretan scribe recast the mundane catalog, giving expression to that conviction."

Even in their brief, monograph format,* Utterbock's assertions have begun to challenge scholars to rethink not just Bronze Age archaeology, but its writings and religion as well. The "reread" inventories may prove to be, in Phillipides's estimation, "the most significant advance in bovinology since Kalistos's identification of the *tauroboleum* as a birth rite." But even if that hope proves extravagant, religious historians are intrigued, and not a little apprehensive, about his suggestion that the huge Cretan goblet industry supported the ritual needs of a "wine into blood" cult. Mythologists do not know quite what to make of his characterization of Ariadne as a Mother Goddess. And literary critics of all stripes recognize the heuristic value of his "unmasking" approach. "What once was boring is now delightful," said a *TLS* reviewer of Utterbock's achievement. "With this deep-song approach to pedestrian writing, even shopping lists become arousing."

The Clippings Oracle (ca. 1000 B.C.)

Fon Ling the Elder

This ingenious book of ancient divination explains the ritualistic cutting and analysis of nail clippings. Written by the so-called manicurist philosopher Fon Ling—whose formula for cuticle removal is, of course, still with us—it is composed of an elaborate "liturgy" to be recited while removing the fingernails and an equally detailed system for reading the future from the positions that the nail clippings assume when they are dropped into a sacred container.

---

* The complete inventories will be brought out by Oxford Press, probably in the spring of 1994. Advance orders are being taken now, and subscribers who prepay before 1990 will receive with their volume an authenticated facsimile of a Linear B shard.

Archaeological evidence hints strongly that both this container (*wei-wei*) and the ceremonial knife (*z'iip*) that figured in the paring ritual were manufactured and sold by Fon Ling himself, and as a result many Chinese—beginning in the oracle's own time and continuing to the present day—have dismissed it as a commercial ploy. Judging from the sophistication of the system, this is a hasty conclusion. Fon Ling may have profited materially from his system, but his text is nonetheless a spiritual classic.

Its brilliance rests chiefly on its exhaustiveness. The *wei-wei* contained five pairs of compartments, providing one receptacle each for the ten fingers' clippings. Each clipping could land in one of four basic patterns, thus: $(\;) \; \cap \; \cup$, with clippings that landed at an eccentric angle being "rounded" to the horizontal or the vertical. This meant that each pair of clippings could fall in a total of sixteen different patterns, and that the total number of patterns for the two hands' worth of clippings was 16^5 or 1,048,576. It was the indefatigable manicurist's great achievement to have provided a pithy, one-line reading for all these possibilities.

With over a million readings to provide, Fon Ling wisely put a premium on brevity. Pattern 69, for example, gives "The dog that trots around finds a bone." Pattern 4099 gives "A stone is stuck in between my toes." Pattern 789,007 gives "Never trust anyone with a tattoo on his face." Pattern 1,009,884 gives "Still waters—they stink." The "Originator" Pattern 1, where all the fallen crescents are "open" to the heavens, gives "Oh, wow, you lucky bastard!" And the "leaden" number 524,288 gives, conversely, "Banana peel."

The book was banned during the short-lived, paranoid Misty dynasty because it was thought that several of the readings referred to the vanity of courtiers. Pattern 87,880, for example, which reads, "You cannot pick your nose with a sword," was taken as a reference to imperial nail guards, and indeed the "shielded" long-nail custom became entrenched in Fon Ling's day because rulers feared their clippings would be used in "black divination" by adepts in the manicurist's service. The ban was not officially lifted until

1953, in the famous Maoist proclamation "I'll pick my nose any way I want if it furthers the glorious revolution."

A modern footnote: Many of the "prophecies" that one finds in Chinese restaurant fortune cookies today—attributed conventionally and wrongly to Confucius—appeared originally in Fon Ling's "aphoristicon." The shape of the cookies as well recollects his industriousness: today's fortune cookie is the confectionary vestige of a nail-biting cult for which Fon Ling provided "special order" readings. Cult members consumed "crescents within crescents" (magic clippings baked inside of pastry) as a way of "locking in" the fortunes they had cast. Paper messages replaced the nails around A.D. 1500, and until only about a hundred years ago, as a way of showing respect for Fon Ling's system, it was customary to eat the message along with the sweet.

The Guniad (8th Century B.C.)

Toto

Although Homer's *Iliad* is the locus classicus for the history of the Trojan War, many famous elements of the story—including Achilles's heel and the wooden horse—do not appear there. They were added to the Homeric account a century after the blind poet's death, and appear only in the comprehensive *Guniad*, by the Balkan rhapsodist Toto. So complete a catalog of Trojaniana is this poem that the Greco-Roman expression *Est in Toto* ("It's in Toto") was a byword for ripeness or completion; the pidginized Latin *in toto* is a survival of that maxim.

For two centuries *The Guniad* was known as the "real" *Iliad*; it only lost its preeminence in the sixth century, when the Athenian tyrant Pisistratus made Homer official and the Balkan infra dig. Why? Because Toto is "barbaric," meaning unpatriotic. *Guniad* means "the women's tale," and the theme is female amusement at male pretension.

The protagonists are Paris's captive Helen, the Amazon queen Penthesilea, the slave girl Briseis, and a Trojan princess named Dot. In Homer, Agamemnon's taking of Briseis from Achilles causes the hero's famous wrath and subsequent peril for the Greeks. Toto presents that wrath as simple pouting—one hero asks the petulant Achilles, "So you're taking your toys and going home?"—and he makes the real question of the war whether or not Helen, Penthesilea, and Dot can get Briseis away from the Greeks altogether so she can rejoin their kaffeeklatsch. Without "bright Briseis" they are reduced to trading market gossip with the bland, uxorious Andromache.

The charm of the poem—and the reason it was censored—is Toto's satirical twisting of heroic conventions. "Crafty Odysseus" is a con man, squandering ransom drachmas for Briseis in order to get drunk with the "oafish Ajax." The Trojans and Greeks alike are "toy soldiers." And Achilles meets his fate not by Paris's arrow, but by a more mundane route: having mortally wounded Penthesilea, he is posing over her bleeding body when she bites him squarely in the heel.

The very cynicism that discredited Toto with the ancients made him posthumously voguish after World War I. The 1920s saw a reassessment of his importance in a study that remains a standard today: C. V. Praxiteles's *Troys in the Attic*. For a less favorable, more conventional view, see Homer B. Homer, "Notes on the Gooniad," in his *The Pisistratean Achievement*.

Zeus's Triplets *(429 B.C.)*

Epididemos

A contemporary of Euripides, Epididemos wrote at least nineteen tragedies and a vast number of satyr plays. As was the case with more famous Greek tragedians, most of the texts have been lost. Fragments of a satyr play called *Bones for Hermes* are preserved in the Ashmolean archives, and the full text of a rather dull *Oedipus and the Sphinx* occasionally finds its way into "second pressing" collections of minor dramatists. But one accomplished work does survive: the trilogy that he himself called "Blunders of Zeus," but that the modern world knows as *Zeus's Triplets*.

The three plays, which were produced as a unit in 429, concern the notorious randiness of the "father god" Zeus. In a story that Epididemos probably made up (no other source gives a version), Zeus rapes the daughter of a wine seller, and she bears three sons with never-ending afflictions: around the clock, Garkos belches, Rippelytos hiccups, and Snafax sneezes. The individual plays follow the three brothers as they search for cures,* curse their fate, and hide from Zeus—who has vowed to kill them for embarrassing him. Protected by Hera (who is quite happy to have her adulterous

---

* The trilogy is particularly interesting to the paleopharmacologist because of its references to ancient folk remedies. See Andrée Nolen, *Hangovers, Hiccups, and Hives: Old Wives' Cures Through the Ages.*

husband embarrassed), each manages to escape his wrath, and is "cured" by being turned into a *memento erotis*. Garkos becomes a bullfrog, Rippelytos a rabbit, and Snafax a woodpecker—all embodiments of lust in ancient folklore.

Because Zeus is clearly the villain in these plays, and Hera the champion of justice, Epididemos has often been seen as a defender of marriage—the "mouthpiece of monogamy," as British Hellenist Coral Griffith quipped. This probably puts more weight on the plays than they should bear, for the writing is more ribald than puritanical, and it seems likely that the author's chief intention was to offer less a sermon than a vulgar romp. His audience certainly appreciated the trilogy in that manner: it received the official 429 *prix d'acclame* as well as a special, ad hoc "phallos garland."

Unfortunately for Epididemos, the archon that year was the paranoid Kruton, and he was convinced by the playwright's jealous rivals that Zeus represented him. Forced to choose between ostracism and the sword, Epididemos took the former and spent the remainder of his days in a Calabrian colony.

To the student of Greek culture, Epididemos is chiefly interesting because of his unusual view of Fate, or Moira. In all three plays Moira is a young woman who, she claims, has "no control

over others—and certainly not over that horny graybeard, the one who uses his member as a scepter." Her debates about morality with Garkos, Snafax, and especially Rippelytos reveal a mind not at all comfortable with the notion that "Fate conquers all." To Moira, Zeus is the very definition of hubris—yet "he gets away with it, every time." "The Epididemean concept of justice," argued Matthew Arnold, "is an affront to the notion of Hellenic balance. If Fate itself does obeisance to passion, then where shall I place my lever, where shall I stand?" Arnold's confusion has been echoed in many readers. No doubt it helps to explain the author's neglect in our time, when the Greeks are commonly displayed as masters of "harmony."

The Death of Aeschylus (mid-4th Century B.C.)

Chrisko

According to legend, the great Athenian dramatist Aeschylus died when a nearsighted eagle mistook his bald head for a rock and dropped a turtle on it, intending to crack the shell. This story generated the Mediterranean superstition against serving turtle soup to playwrights (this is still taken seriously in Sicily, where Aeschylus died), and it also led to one of the ancient world's true philosophical satires, Chrisko's "dialogue" *The Death of Aeschylus*.

Born at Corinth into a metalworker's family, Chrisko left for Athens about 360 B.C. to follow the teachings and errant ways of Diogenes's Cynics. A favorite pupil of the "Athenian Thoreau," he is said to have made the tub in which Diogenes slept, and to have been the silent collaborator on many aphorisms. Saul Gaspard's contention that he actually ghosted all of Diogenes's sayings is tantalizing but unprovable, and I am inclined, with most classicists, to accept their relationship as one of fruitful exchange rather than mutual theft.

Certainly the two men were kindred souls, sharing an aversion to pomposity and particularly to the formal philosophy of their day. Compare, for example, Diogenes's much-quoted remark that he had seen Plato's cup and table but not his "tableness" or "cupness" (a sly dig at the theory of forms) with Chrisko's definition of Aristotelian logic as "the act of proving to a bird that it can fly."

Chrisko's snaps at Aristotle are copiously displayed in *The Death of Aeschylus*, which he subtitled "a saurian complaint." The speakers of the play are the eagle and the tortoise, and far from indulging in the Aesopian banter one would expect from such a cast, they rattle on incessantly about teleology. In Aristotle's view, each living creature developed naturally (unless artificially impeded) toward its own "true" or "mature" nature: thus the tadpole achieved its fullness as a frog, and no wine should be sold before its time. The captured turtle plays mercilessly with this doctrine, questioning whether, for example, the bird's nestlings might not become more truly "aquiline" if they were fed on field mice and stolen fish; and whether it isn't really a turtle's "nature" to end up "swimming in a scallion and oregano broth."

The answers to these puzzles never come because the eagle drops his prize on the playwright's head, and the turtle is reduced to fitful splutters: "Whoa! Omigod, I'm flying! Is that destiny I see bobbing? That's the whitest rock I've ever seen." There's a deafening crash (given by the Greek onomatopoeia *Duwop Shiboom!*—which means roughly "Heads up! Too late!"), and the eagle swoops down for his meal, only to find that the turtle has escaped, leaving him with the dead writer's fractured cranium. With a plaintive aside to the audience (incidentally a *hapax legomenon* in Greek literature), he asks the question that has become known as "Chrisko's Conundrum": "Athenian brains or turtle meat, what's the difference?"

Because of stylistic affinities between this play and Aristotle's own lost exoteric writings, Stagira Chalcidich has claimed that Aristotle himself wrote it—a "gesture of humorous complicity with his Cynic critics." Since nothing else in Aristotle is the least bit funny, this must be taken as Macedonian special pleading of the grossest order. See Tesla Gavotte's chapter, "The Chrisko Kid," in his soon-to-be-translated *Archaeische Funkmeisters*, for a debunking of this ludicrous thesis.

The Martyr (385 B.C.)

Koriander

No figure in Western thought is more revered than the Athenian gadfly Socrates. Thanks to the laudatory dialogues of his most famous pupil, Plato, the Greek philosopher comes down to us as the prototype of the professional thinker: diligent, impartial, and so dedicated to truth that even death cannot quench his allegiance. This image has endured for 2500 years, and even Aristophanes's parody in *The Clouds* has made little break in the tradition—it is conventionally dismissed as comic hyperbole.

But Aristophanes was not the only ancient who found Plato's piety disgusting. Fifteen years after the philosopher's execution on a charge of corrupting the morals of Athenian minors, his less celebrated pupil Koriander published a monologue entitled *The Martyr*, which used the master's own motto, "Know yourself," to reexamine both his doctrines and his "selflessness." Charles William Eliot called the monologue "a tendentious beef by a C-minus student with an ax to grind," and it is unfortunate that this dismissive attitude has endured, for Koriander's vision is both credible and provocative. Rather than ridiculing the Socratic teachings, he accepts them wholeheartedly, but "doubts the doubter" by questioning his sincerity. What to Plato was selflessness, Koriander characterizes as self-advertisement of a particularly disingenuous variety. To Plato, Socrates's ascetic garb, his refusal to take payment for his teaching, and, most of all, his acceptance of judicial death, all pointed to his obeisance to Higher Ideals. Koriander saw not humility but a fretful stabbing at notoriety—a desperate grab for public prominence to which his bland teachings themselves could not entitle him. Or, to put it in the pithy language for which *The Martyr* is well known, "Even goat meat may be appetizing if cooked in ouzo."

Not that Koriander considers Socrates insincere. On the contrary, he makes it clear that the philosopher's commitment to truth was profound. He understood—certainly better than Plato—that to a nation which had just weathered a debilitating war, shock tactics were perfectly in order: only they would seem true. In addition, he understood that his fellow citizens would remember his words longer if they were bathed in the afterglow of his blood. Hence his self-sacrifice on the altar of wisdom.

Socrates's willingness to die for the truth, therefore, should be seen not as a tragic necessity, but as the last element of a calculated effort to make his words ring longer than those of the Sophists. It was not that he despised worldly fame, but that he wanted his own to outlive him. In this sense, of course, he resembled the Western tradition's second Great Teacher, the fiercely (and publicly) humble Jesus of Nazareth.

The majority of philosophic critics since Socrates's day have endorsed Plato's narrow view of the master. One notable exception is Berna Dietrickover, whose recent translation of Koriander's collected works—including a wonderfully somber version of his satyr play *Aristotle and Phyllis*—corrects a millennia-old misunderstanding. Dietrickover is especially illuminating on the "irregularities" at Plato's academy that caused Koriander's expulsion and subsequent literary revenge.

The Dice Game (2nd Century B.C.)

Steverinus

Ostensibly a "philosophical" drama modeled on Plato's *Symposium*, Steverinus's only surviving play actually punctures Socratic pretensions by putting philosophy in the mouths of pompous fools. The setting of the play is a dice game, or *alea*, at the villa of the gambler Ophidoculus. He has promised a prize of five hundred *sestertii* to anyone who can best him at *tabula* (a forerunner of backgammon), and the drama recounts the attempt of four takers: the *miles gloriosus* Rambobiceps, probably modeled on Julius Caesar; the Spanish ambassador Garbanzo, almost certainly modeled on Cicero (both names translate as "chick pea"); the Stoic philosopher Ponderus, who has been called "a Marcus Aurelius with a beer gut"; and a mendicant Cynic, "The Tub," who is Steverinus's nod to Diogenes.

While they vie for the prize, they argue philosophy. Rambobiceps boasts about *fama*, claiming, "I will live forever, I will learn how to fly." Garbanzo praises *justicia*, and as a demonstration of its value describes how order improved in his province once he crucified sixty-five slaves. Ponderus dotes on his mistress Sophia, a gladiator groupie who has come to Ophidoculus's only because the arena is closed for repairs. The Tub slings mud at the company, picks his nose ostentatiously, sneezes uproariously, and attempts to fondle Sophia. The host sits quietly by, defeating each of the foursome in turn and awarding the prize to Sophia "because she had the good sense not to babble."

In its affront to ancient sophistry, *The Dice Game* may be likened to Aristophanes; the Ponderus character in particular suggests the basket-dwelling Socrates of *The Clouds*. But its meter and vulgar topicality make it Roman—the quality that appealed to Alexander Pope's rival Lane Drury, who turned its "streetwise" language into London slang. The opening line of Act II, for example, is *Alea jactanda est*, or "The die must be cast"; Drury's 1719 version reads, "Damn yer eyes, man, throw them bones!"

Steverinus also wrote epodes and, around 15 B.C., a companion play called *The Orgy*. Only one fragmented line survives: "Oh no, Scrofulus, not another toga party! Can't we just stay at home and peel grapes?"

The Art of Stuffing *(1st Century B.C.)*

Bulimius

In the same period that Ovid was writing the *Ars Amatoria*, his younger contemporary Bulimius was producing another paean to excess, the *Ars Farcienda*, or "Art of Stuffing." Like Ovid's classic, Bulimius's explores a patrician pastime as a way of chiding imperial decadence; but while Ovid was sophisticated and discreet, Bulimius used the idiomatic Pompeiian "gutter" language popularized by his friend Attica XVI. This tended to obscure his work later on, and it is only in our democratic century that Bulimius is beginning to regain an audience.

The *Ars Farcienda* is divided into three books. The first is a tribute to Roman dining that includes detailed descriptions of famous banquets—among them the notorious "soliloquy feast" at which Lucullus was said to have dined alone. The Victorian repugnance at Roman decadence owes much to his praise of larks' tongue soup, and our understanding of Roman cuisine comes largely from the poet's "grocery lists."

In the second book, Bulimius presents his famous formulas for successful *noctes farciendae*, or "nights of stuffing." Playing on the popular Lucretian philosophy, he computes the number of atoms of food that must be consumed, per minute per diner, for the host to earn the coveted title of *fartor*, or "fattener"; he also gives a formula for a *semifartor*, rustic slang for a pig boy. And he presents weighty evidence—including "Pythagorean" equations—that Lucullus deserves the unique title Fartor Maximus.

In the final book, Bulimius satirizes the Roman practice of inducing nausea in order to make room for more food. Seneca's maxim *Vomunt ut edant, edunt ut vomant* ("Vomit to eat, eat to vomit") was lifted from this popular section. The third book is also notable for an exhaustive catalog of ancient purgatives (including an unidentified substance known as *ipecacca*) and for an "underground gourmet's street guide" to the most interesting Roman vomitoria.

Practically nothing is known of Bulimius. The *Farcienda* mentions only his birth year (32 B.C.) and his fondness for the grape. There is a Tuscan legend that he attempted to introduce the "poisonous" eggplant into Italy and was stoned to death as a result. But a recent translator of the *Farcienda*, Mlle. Andrée Gregoire of the Sorbonne, calls this tale "typical Etruscan balderdash."

The Tenth Muse (1st Century)

"Saltus"

The dance crazes of the late Middle Ages—including the tarantella, the St. Vitus episodes, and the various Dances of Death—have been amply documented; this is not the case with a Roman precursor of these phenomena that was created virtually single-

handedly by a visionary versifier known as "Saltus." He lived at
the height of the so-called Jaded Era, when patricians had become
weary of gladiatorial contests and were ripe for a new form of
amusement. Saltus provided it with enormous gusto, first in his
poem "The Tenth Muse" and then in a public display of the poem's
underlying theme.

That theme, as stated at the outset, was that nine muses were
not enough, and that an addition to the traditional pantheon should
be created, in the person of the "forgotten goddess Pogo." As she
was presented by Saltus—his name means "The Leaper"—Pogo
was a creature of prodigious energy, whose delight was what a
later age would call "gamboling," and whose mortal prototypes
were woodland nymphs fleeing the rapacious Pan. If festivals hon-
oring the "official" goddess of dance, Chorea, were sedate, formal
affairs, the celebrations that Saltus proposed to honor Pogo were
frenzied and irregular in the extreme: the point of a Pogo-inspired
dance, Saltus explained, was to be "constantly out of step."

To demonstrate the ecstatic value of this type of activity, Saltus
himself, in the year 41, "danced" his way from the Forum to the
port of Ostia—a distance of about twenty miles—to the great en-
joyment of assembled crowds. It took him a day and a half because
his choreographic style was so erratic: in keeping with the tenth
muse's saltic preferences, the poet leaped continually up and down,
advancing toward Ostia by small increments and causing one spec-
tator, the rival poet Bimbo, to describe him as a "bouncing reed."

Saltus's popularity as a traveling sideshow continued for about
five years, but the effect of his whimsical poem lasted longer. The
great Hungarian neodeconstructionist Tesla Gavotte claims that it
actually created the tarantella craze, through the ministry of the
Italian scholar Giovanni Frug, who published a vernacular edition
in 1510. Students established a Pogo Memorial Society at Verona
around 1520, and even today Saltus remains a Veronese folk hero.
Beyond the Alps, too, his influence survives. "The Tenth Muse"
is still a cult classic to professional acrobats in the Low Countries,
northern Germany, and parts of France.

Works and Days (2nd Century)

Agorides

Often referred to as "the poor man's Plutarch," this tableau of common people's daily lives shared a titular and a mundane affinity with Hesiod's work, but was as urban and unassuming as Hesiod's had been rural and didactic. The son of a Salonika fruitseller, Agorides (his name means literally "child of the marketplace") saw his warm, detailed survey of everyday life as a homage to the simple folk of his native town. In his lifetime Plutarch's "parallel lives" had already begun to gather fame, and Agorides meant to augment the Chaeronean's "museum of moral lessons" (as he describes it in his preface) by "singing not of generals already sung, but of those who made their sandals and their wine."

Works and Days thus contains some fifty sketches of the forgotten men and women of northern Greece. Cobblers and vintners, weavers and shepherds, sailmakers and temple prostitutes and household slaves—a panoply of the Aegean working class speaks here of its everyday concerns, with its own ribald imagery and its own slang. The slang vocabulary has always been a boon for scholars, since Plutarch and other erudite writers rely on hieratic, "proper" jargon, which uses the limited vocabulary of the privileged classes. Because Agorides's speakers use a first person "gutter demotic," his collection provides invaluable information about vowel shifting in this critical period, especially on the Macedonian plateau. Marios Anarchiades, the Thracian expert on Indo-European comparative morphology, calls Agorides "the virtual wellspring of our knowledge. Without him we would be in the ridiculous condition of supposing that Alexander and his barber sounded alike."

Social historians have been equally fond of Works and Days. Joan Powys, whose exemplary social history Medieval People recounts the "daily histories" of French peasants and prioresses, admits that she used Agorides as a model: "He is the first historian who can also be called a sociologist. He saw that society was dirty fingernails, not just purple robes." Billings Wade, in his four-volume survey *Daily Life in Ancient Times*, ranks him as "a better observer of detail even than Tacitus. If we wish to know precisely how a second-century Greek tied his sandal, or painted tiles, or prepared dolmades, we have no better source than the sage of Salonika."

Philosophically, Agorides disclaimed allegiance to any school, yet he has generally been accounted a Stoic, and with reason. If there is a single mood that pervades the voices of his fifty speakers, it is one of dignified, calm acceptance. There are no revolutionaries here, no disgruntled social climbers or scheming slaves, but only, as Alexander Pope commented, "each man in his place, and a place for all." With the exception of an occasional Marxist ideologue, readers have found this mood compelling. Marcus Aurelius spoke for generations to come when he punned, in a fugitive passage of his *Meditations*, "*Aliquando vox populi vox agorae dei.*"

A History of the Vanquished (240)

Romulus Africanus

The third century of the Christian era was a frantically dismal one for ancient Rome. Taxation, military adventure, and inflation all undermined domestic tranquillity, and the resulting atmosphere of malaise was fueled by class conflict, foreign threats, and—perhaps most telling of all—a fusion of the frivolous and the macabre whose chief evidence was the cult of the arena. Far from checking this erosion of stability, the emperors actually encouraged it by a policy of bread and circuses (generally more of the latter than the former), until many of them became its most famous victims. Between the accession of Caracalla in 211 and that of Constantine in 306, thirty rulers "governed" the Empire, and the vast majority left the throne by assassination.

It is against the backdrop of this mismanaged majesty that we must view the work of the black Roman, Romulus (or, as he preferred to be called, Remus) Africanus. Born a slave near the site of ancient Carthage, he was the house servant of the African proconsul Sextus Verrus until 218, when that percipient individual, recognizing the boy's linguistic talent, sent him as a translator to Rome. With a knowledge of Greek, Latin, and Numidian, the seventeen-year-old quickly made himself useful to the imperial court, and by the time he was twenty he had acquired from visiting legations additional facility in Persian and Urgermanisch. In 241 he bought his freedom—an unusual achievement at a time when the demand for slaves was increasing—and turned his learning skills to other purposes. Supporting himself as a tutor, he composed in the next fifteen years the remarkable "antihistory" that made him (in Gladys Knight's words) "the Gibbon who was actually there."

Romulus Africanus's *Populorum Historia Vinctorum*, or "History of the Vanquished," is remarkable not only for its varied moods—ranging from the elegiac to the flippant—but also because its basic premise repudiated traditional historiography. From Herodotus down to Suetonius, history had been the tale of the triumphant: Greece's victory over Persia, Rome's over Gaul, and so on. Romulus shifted the focus, giving his readers in seven pungent chapters the *pictura in conspectu mortuorum*, or the "view in the eyes of the dead." Thus we hear Xerxes on the Battle of Salamis, Hannibal's version of Zama, Vercingetorix's lament over the loss of Gaul to Julius Caesar, and—in one of the history's defter jabs at imperial arrogance—the Persian Darius III's railings at the depredations of the Macedonian marvel, Alexander Pusillus (Alexander the Puny).

Romulus might have gotten away with this potentially subversive satire had he not tipped his hand baldly in the final chapter. There, adopting the persona of "Remus," the first loser of the Roman tradition, he narrates the doleful history of his own time, denouncing the barbarians crouched across the Danube in the same tone that his Hannibal had denounced Rome. The implication was clear: the Romans, too, whatever their current pretensions, were soon to become *populi vincti*. No wonder Edward Gibbon called Romulus "prescient," and no wonder his own people found him troubling. Emperor Gordian III was so troubled that he condemned Romulus first to house arrest and then to the arena. He escaped only by fleeing to Asia, where, according to legend, he wrote *rubaiyat* for the Persian court until his death around 250.

The Persian sections of the African's opus have often been collected under the title *Achaemenidian*, while the contemporary (that is, second-century) chapter has been translated as *The Testament of Remus*. Eurocentric publishing bias has scotched at least three attempts at a full English translation, the most famous being John Dryden's.

Odovacar's Dream (488)

Futhark

Odovacar is known to historians as the man who finished off the Roman Empire. On August 28, 476, he deposed the child emperor Romulus Augustus and thereupon became the first—though hardly the last—barbarian king of greater Italy. He ruled the territory quietly for a dozen years, modestly trimming the bureaucracy, introducing the Christmas tree to the Christianized Romans, and then—in his one serious error—threatening the Byzantine emperor Zeno by invading Dalmatia in 488. In response, Zeno enlisted the king of the Ostrogoths, Theodoric, to drive Odovacar from his doorstep and from Rome. The sad results of that invitation are related—or rather foretold—in this remarkable "premonitory history" by the scribe Futhark.

The dream of the title is one Odovacar has on the night that he hears of Zeno's move—sometime in the summer of 488. In it, he sees himself as a king of Babylon, the biblically celebrated potentate Belshazzar, in whose banquet hall a mysterious hand foretells his demise. Belshazzar/Odovacar sees a similar hand, only it is wearing the traditional "ring of power" of Gothic warlords, and the message that it writes is less ambiguous than the *"Mene mene tekel upharsin"* of the Book of Daniel: "Before five summers dies the swan." Born with an unusually elongated neck, Odovacar had always been known as "the Swan," and he takes the dream to be a portent of his death. He's right. Less than five years later, on March 15, 493, Theodoric kills him.

There would be nothing remarkable about this if the story had *followed* the ruler's death: there are plenty of examples in literary history of astonishing "predictions" being recorded after the fact. But Futhark wrote the tale by 490—we know this because the hand is clearly his, and because he died in that year during an epidemic. Alexander Yarrowville's famous attempt to show that the scribe's grave marker had been faked by "augury mongers" has long ago been discredited by reputable scholars,* and so we are left with Odovacar's painful knowledge and an air of still unexplained mystery.

The mystery is deepened by Futhark's own emendations. His description of the haunted Odovacar slaughtering captives to pro-

---

* Yarrowville has few supporters today, but his speculations are still enchantingly derisive. See especially his undergraduate essay in Foster Keele's *Brattlestreet Bagatelles*, "Chronometric Inanities in Old Norse: or Dates, Nuts, and the Futhark Problem."

pitiate the "masters of doom" did come to pass—as did his prediction that the doomed ruler would be assassinated at a real banquet on the ides of March. The popularity of the volume rests still on the eeriness of these foreshadowings, and even those who dismiss its "occult" significance generally acknowledge—in the words of Old Norse scholar Hilda Beckback—that "there is a mist here that does not quite settle."

Solutions to the puzzle have ranged from the esoteric to the mundane: the so-called Leipzig numerology school makes much of the "death resonance" of 3/15—the date on which both Julius Caesar and Odovacar are assassinated; while the Beckback-backed Cambridge contingent suggests that the king, in a "fit of faith," committed suicide rather than offend the masters of doom he so feared.

The Gascon Chronicle (ca. 800)

Eskaduin

The most famous of chansons de geste, the eleventh-century *Chanson de Roland*, celebrates the bravery of Charlemagne's nephew Roland and his death in a Saracen ambush. In the actual battle on which the poem was based, however, the enemy were not Arabs but Gascons—the ancestors of today's Basques—and in *The Gascon Chronicle*, which appeared only twenty-two years after the event, we get a rather different view of what happened than the conventional (that is, Frankish) one.

In the Gascon poet Eskaduin's version, Charlemagne is the villain, and his "armored lapdogs" Roland and Oliver (whom he calls Rolli and Olli) bring destruction down on themselves in furthering the emperor's grand design—the subjugation of all western Europe. When the Gascons balk at this imperialistic fantasy, Rolli and Olli "torch their fields and slay their sheep so that the Pig King to the north may smack his lips."

Understandably upset at the Frankish incursion, the Gascons take up arms to drive the invaders back, slaying Rolli, Olli, and their companions in the famous fight at Roncevaux Pass. Eskaduin's description of that battle is less sentimental and more exuberant than the Frankish version, expressing about the same sympathy for the slain as the Sioux version of Custer's last stand. Roland's soldiers, says the poet, fight "only fiercely enough to vanquish mutton; they are not in the habit of slaying men." (This particular point is Gascon boasting. To demonstrate the magnanimity of imperial authority, Charlemagne's stalwarts once slaughtered four thousand Saxons in one day.)

The reversal at Roncevaux notwithstanding, Charlemagne did extend his sway over Europe, and on Christmas Day, 800, the Pope crowned him Emperor of the West. Eskaduin sent a copy of his poem to Rome as a coronation present, which gives an idea of his sense of humor. That sense also permeates the epic, appearing most notoriously in the battle scene where Rolli tries to blow his horn to summon aid and discovers that he does not remember how: his dying words, as he is felled by a Gascon spear, are "I knew I should have kept up with those lessons."

The Gascon poet's satirical thrusts at the Franks are unrelenting. Charlemagne is continually called the Pig King because he "roots forward, with his tail in the air." His soldiers are, collectively, "the imperialist swine," "the trash barons," or simply "scum." And the Frankish leader's Holy Roman Empire is, in Eskaduin's dismissive taunt, "neither holy, Roman, nor an empire." Generations of college freshman have recited this formula, of course, without ever knowing where it came from.

The official neglect afforded Eskaduin's work is testimony not only to Frankish suppression, but to the eleventh-century interest in Arab bashing. With Christian Europe gearing up for the Crusades, a poem about Frenchmen versus Basques was of marginal political utility. Thus Eskaduin's countrymen were transformed into Saracens, and the sheep slayers became "most Christian knights."

The Rotenaksaga (10th Century)

Anonymous

The Icelandic sagas are prose epics with a decidedly heroic cast. The typical protagonist is a warrior; the sensibility is that of stern courage; the plot turns on fate and dire vengeance. Humor figures occasionally in the brief *thaettir*, or tales, that were told in the same period of lesser mortals, but in the longer productions it is rare; the sagas unfold in a rarefied realm of implacable fate and grave silence. A notable exception is the burlesque *Rotenaksaga*.

The epic is the tale of arrogant Rotenak, a hunter who sees himself as a hero, or (as some have claimed) a bungler who sees himself as a god. In this rollicking parody of the Norse warrior's life, Rotenak displays appropriate virtues—daring, self-confidence, stolidity in the face of disaster—but he displays them to such self-destructive lengths that the epic moves, like the hero himself, toward a reductio ad absurdum.

Rotenak displays his penchant for excess even as a child. Having heard the tale of young Hercules from a bard who has been to the continent, the youngster goes searching for serpents so he may strangle them as the Greek hero did in his cradle. Since there are no snakes in Iceland, this proves a fruitless venture, and he contents himself with stepping on earthworms and then bragging about the feat to his friends. As a young man he engages in further stupidities: eating fifty eggs at one sitting (and claiming he has devoured fifty chickens); breaking every bone in his body while trying to climb the great World Tree; and developing a debilitating case of "lancer's elbow" in trying to hurl his spear to the moon.

Through most of this inanity, Rotenak is protected by the indulgent goddess Freya, who has a soft spot for him because he reminds her of her equally trying cousin, the trickster god Loki: she reassembles him after the tree mishap, for example, and replaces his head on another occasion when it's bitten off by the dragon Merlhaggard. But when he challenges Freya herself, he meets his match. Boasting that he can endure an Icelandic night unclothed, he is brought in the next morning "rigid as Doom." (I have indicated elsewhere that this gave us the taunt "Last one in is a rotten egg.")

Rotenak is a well-known folk figure in Scandinavia, but academics have largely ignored him because his behavior is at variance with saga formula. Alfred Dante does give him a brief mention in his study of the Berserkers, *Rambo and Odin*, and Snorri Snorrelson, of the Reykjavik Archives, has published an appreciative note in *Scandinavian Folklore*, but the world still awaits a full-length study and a serviceable English translation. Richmond Wesley's suggestion, in his recent article "Cool Hand Loki," that the saga was the sacred text of a "Loki cult," is not worth serious consideration.

Banquet at Canossa *(1080)*

Matilda of Tuscany

The principal political issue of eleventh-century Europe was the conflict between the Holy Roman Empire and the papacy over who really bossed the German church. Emperor Henry IV, citing traditional feudal bonds, claimed that German bishops owed their power to him. Not so, said Pope Gregory VII: episcopal power came from Rome, and Henry appointed (or "invested") bishops only at the pleasure of the Holy See. The resulting Investiture Controversy nearly cost Henry his throne; he only salvaged it by acknowledging Gregory's primacy in 1076, with his famous "barefoot in the snow" penance at Canossa.

European history holds few tableaux more vivid than the picture of Henry awaiting Gregory's forgiveness outside the walls of the Tuscan castle. But to judge from *Banquet at Canossa*, it was nothing to what was going on inside. Since Gregory was extremely anxious for Henry's capitulation, medievalists have never been quite sure why he forced Henry to wait three full days (risking a volte-face) before granting him absolution. Matilda's account explains why: he was too occupied with her (the castle's mistress) to be distracted by a mere emperor.

Matilda did not say bluntly that she and Gregory "dallied" while Henry fumed. She didn't have to. The term *banchetto*, in eleventh-century Italian, was a common euphemism for a sexual escapade, and the culinary details in *Il banchetto a Canossa*—there is much talk of lip smacking and "steaming" thighs—made her meaning perfectly clear. The only question is why the so-called Grand Countess—long the *suspected* mistress of the pope—should have chosen to reveal herself in this manner. To that question historians have given two answers.

The contemporary explanation was simple revenge. Imprisoned as a girl by Henry's father, Matilda had no affection for the emperor, and it is reasonable to suppose she issued her *confessio amantis* as a way of adding insult to injury: an audacious flaunting of the fact that, even while enjoining celibacy on Henry's clerics, Gregory himself was above the law. The more modern explanation sees the book as, in Otto Staufen's terms, "a veiled confession matching Henry's own." "It was her own way of doing penance," Staufen wrote, "of begging forgiveness for her well-known sexual gluttony."

Whichever explanation is correct, *Il banchetto* remains a fascinating model of medieval allegory, as deftly ribald as the tales of the *Decameron* (whose author acknowledged Matilda's influence) and as rigorous in its working-out of analogies as anything in Langland or Alec of Yarrow. Indeed, Irish historian Terence Hoote finds the food-sex parallels "so obsessively exact" that he calls the countess "as obviously a closet logician as a public whore."

With the Investiture Controversy long forgotten, there have been attempts to read Matilda's text "straight," as simply a cookbook. This revisionist approach, however banal, has had one salutary effect: we now have the original Tuscan recipes for *saltimbocca* and *naso del papa*.

Baron Schmutzik and the Knights of the Pit (12th Century?)

"Gustavus von Aachenbach"

In 1651, at an estate liquidation in Lower Upper Westphalia, the heirs of Heinrich Johanissimus Graf von Thundertentronckh offered for sale a yellowed parchment which they claimed was a thirteenth-century copy of a twelfth-century "von Aachenbach" text *aus alterer Zeit*, that is, of indeterminate age. The date of this curious prose poem, like the identity of the author, has puzzled scholars ever since. The vocabulary is clearly Altdeutsch, suggesting a date no later than 1300, but its syntax is out of joint for that period (the preponderance of the subjunctive in itself indicates a fourteenth- or even fifteenth-century origin), while the recurrent phrases *Donnerkriege* (thunder wars) and *Feuerstücke* (fire pieces) have struck many as gunnery references—which argues for no earlier than 1600. Ordnance expert Bartrand Fievel, in fact, calls the work "an extended allegory, a virtual blow-by-blow account of the Thirty Years' War." The real Aachenbach, he believes, was Thundertentronckh himself—an amateur gunsmith and known prankster.

The ambience and the plot line are medieval enough. The protagonist, a peasant named Schmutzik, serves a heartless master for twenty years and then, when the old man dies, finds himself suddenly wealthy: the guilty geezer has left him his estate. Overnight the peasant becomes a *grand seigneur*. He moves his family into the manor house, invites twelve fellow peasants to be his entourage, and begins calling himself the Graf von Schmutzik. The poem's satire arises from social blunders that reveal his earnest foolishness to be a universal, not a personal, affliction. In the best tradition of the German *Naar*, Schmutzik exposes others' inanity through his own.

One device makes the point well. Following the example of the "great Teuton duke, Arturus of Britain," Schmutzik begins to hold roundtable meetings, at which he assigns tasks to his "vassals" as required proofs of their valor. The meetings are held under a banner inscribed *Bleibe der Erde treu* ("Remain true to the earth") in an abandoned ash pit that the "Baron" finds "as homey as mother's womb." The tasks are as earthy as the sunken "table." One knight must plant heather on the Brocken mountain; a second must go fishing for carp; a third must help a local midwife feed her chickens, and so on. Much of the manuscript is the story of such adventures.

Early readers of *Baron Schmutzik* took it as a send-up of medieval epics, a reductio ad absurdum of chivalric ideals. Since the invention of "deep reading" in the last century, however, the poem has been yielding richer clues. W. H. Roscher and other "naturist" writers claimed in the 1880s that Schmutzik was a vestigial earth deity, the modern residue of an ancient *Erdhölle*, or "hole in the ground" cult. Historian Wybald Becher, in a famous monograph on the Wars of Religion, depicted "Aachenback" as a "latent Anabaptist," urging a purified, "grounded" theology as a counter to "hieratic Romish elaborations." And the psycho-readers, inevitably, seized on Schmutzik's "womb fixation": to them he was "an insufficiently cathected autophant."

Mystifying as he has been to critics, Aachenbach has always pleased his (or her) fellow writers. Grimmelshausen's antihero Simplicissimus and Brecht's outrageously commonsensical judge

Azdak are only the two most obvious copies of the "stupid-smart" peasant baron; while the more recent recasting of the Grail legend by Montgomery Snake obviously relies heavily on Schmutzik's *Pitzerhelden* for its description of the Knights Who Say Nih.

A Concordance to Guillaume de Montmorcy-Burke (1199)

Dudo St. Quentin

Montmorcy-Burke merits a place in literary history on two counts. First, he was the most distinguished Anglo-Norman poet of his generation—a south Kentish equal, his contemporaries agreed, of the Frankish realm's Walter von der Vogelweide. Second, he is the world's only major writer whose works are known only from a concordance.*

Of his succès d'estime there can be no doubt. The Lyon Codex calls him "the modern Orpheus," and notes that when he entered a village to perform, nonce holidays were the rule rather than the exception. Guy Gisbourne, the singer's sometime companion, claimed that his lyrics flowed directly "from God's mouth to Will's ear," and even Henry II, who had every right to execute him for sedition, admitted that "his golden head purleth so close unto an Angel that we fear removing it may be espied as hacking Godde." Two centuries after Montmorcy-Burke's death, Alec of Yarrow still referred to him as "*numerus unus*: a poet for all tymes and all seasons."

---

* The same is true, of course, of the love poetry of "Crazy Jane" Bishop and the Hammer Novels of the Swede Varø Pilquist—but neither can honestly be called a major writer.

This sweet singer's poems are forever gone—casualties of the fourteenth-century vowel shift, when so many lyrics were lost in transit. It is true that several Norman folk songs, including the captivating "Groveling for Dolores," are traditionally ascribed to him, but this has been done on poor authority: the earliest "positive identification" of a Montmorcy-Burke lyric came only in 1809, during the self-serving Kentish revival. Not a single verified line survives.

What does survive is the Dudo concordance—a meticulous word and phrase count completed only two years after the poet's death. Working inferentially from this compilation, we can divine not only Montmorcy-Burke's major themes, but the reasons for his great popularity. His lyrics touched occasionally on the conventional troubadour themes of love and death, but they were also intensely political. In the 893 lines indexed by the Scribe of St. Quentin, there are twelve instances of the catchphrase "swine barons," thirteen of "our good cabbage king" (a poke at Henry II's small head), and twenty of "taxation without representation." In addition there are dozens of references to a "holy" or "blessed" Pastor Smudge, which have been interpreted both as anticlerical invective and as praise of the unwashed poor. Either way, the poet's proto-revolutionary sensibilities are clear. The Spartacist reader Rex Furriner is being only slightly hyperbolic when he calls Montmorcy-Burke a "lutenist Joe Hill."

Scholars have always been puzzled as to why Dudo chose to compile a phrase list instead of transcribing the lyrics themselves. Brendan Coracle's guess that they were so well known as not to need transcription is less helpful than his observation that writing them down would have been pointless for the poet's illiterate audience. Miriam-Luce Charge-Daffaire, taking a sensible psychosocial perspective, supposes that the concordance was a "coded version of the poetry which, had it been transcribed directly, would have implicated the scribe in subversion." The most intriguing theory is a recent one. Writing in *New Middle Age* journal, Exeter Wristgrabbe says that Dudo was a "preincarnation" of today's

Quentin Doud, and that his unusual enterprise was designed "to bequeath to his computer-age counterpart a conundrum that was equal to his talents." Doud himself calls this "highly flattering, but only if we're talking COBOL II."

For the Furriner and Charge-Daffaire theses, see Emily Skifflewacket's masterfully edited *Dudo Renascent: a Festschrift for Brendan Coracle*. For a sample of the St. Quentin manuscript, see Appendix B of this volume.

The Romance of the Flytrap *(ca. 1235)*

Frère Antonanus

The allegorical poem *Roman de la rose*, begun around 1230 by Guillaume de Lorris, was for two hundred years the most widely read book in all Europe. A tale of a forlorn lover's attempt to pluck a single rose from a garden, it became the prototypical handbook of courtly love, was as frequently quoted as the Bible, and generated numerous imitations. Antonanus's contribution, while less well known than Jean de Meung's lengthy continuation or Chaucer's translation, added something to the courtly love tradition that neither of them had imagined: a pervasive spirit of "love terror" to which de Lorris had barely alluded.

Antonanus belonged to the Cathari, and, like all the members of that heretical Languedoc sect, he was violently suspicious of materiality: to the Cathari, salvation lay in renouncing the physical world. This included renouncing sexuality, even of the mildest variety: Antonanus means "against Onan," and it is telling that the monk's early verses describe the "horrible" effects of masturbation (including such supposedly Victorian fantasies as mental debility and marred complexions). His emendation of de Lorris's euphemistic love story betrays that same crabbed sensibility, but with an unusual horticultural twist.

Where de Lorris had used a rose as the emblem of desire, the Cathar monk uses a Venus flytrap—a perfect symbol for Eros turned nasty. Antonanus's lover, too, seeks to remove his "flower" from a garden, but he ends up worse than frustrated: the carnivorous plant devours his hand and is working its way up his arm when the lover, rescued by Pure Feeling, explains that a hand is a small price to pay for the retention of "that most precious jewel, Chastitie."

Many commentators have noted that the central event of this curious *antiroman* evokes the medieval phobia regarding the "vagina indentata," and while this fear seems ridiculous to us, it was not laughable in the thirteenth century. Nor—except for the blatancy of the metaphor—was its bias confined to that time. The devouring woman as a cultural archetype found "civilized" expression as late as Keats's *Lamia*, and Jeffrey Ponds, the eminent British analyst, has even traced the modern male's wariness of commitment to "a subliminal, and quite ancient, absorption paranoia."

The thirteenth century did not need modern psychology, however, to laugh Antonanus out of court. His poem provides a fascinating gloss on courtly love, and on the attitudes of his own sect, but its sensibility was decidedly outré. Rome tolerated its misogyny but found its Manichaeism repugnant, and its brief popularity in the 1230s contributed to Pope Gregory IX's establishment of the Inquisition in the middle of that decade. It can hardly be claimed that the book's subsequent suppression posed a serious threat to Western culture, although from a technical standpoint the text is quite striking: Antonanus's mastery of internal rhyme alone has been compared favorably to Rod McKuen's.

The Grey Book (ca. 1300)

Pietro Cemilo

The various "sorcerer's handbooks" that circulated from the Middle Ages into the so-called Enlightenment were popularly known as Black Books. The Bolognese Cemilo's *Libro Grigio* was designed as a parodistic gloss not only on these serious manuals but also on the Gallic pedantry that supported them. In 1300, the University of Paris—widely known as a center of demonological "study"—was only forty years old, while the University of Bologna was over two hundred; it is widely believed that Cemilo (who taught veterinary law in his native town) meant his book as an interuniversity jibe at the "upstart frogs."

The French *grimoires* or "dark grammars" are filled with spells to summon demons and produce "effects": among the most popular, not surprisingly, were the standbys of romantic conquest and instant wealth. Cemilo played on the predictability of such aspirations by giving prescriptions for the attainment of less obvious goals. The demon Guguais might be summoned, for example, to help the sorcerer "seduce an Abesse or a Bishop." Mikimaus might be enlisted to do household chores like laundry and chopping wood. And the Great Mage of Lent, the demon Copacabana, might be asked for "fiery entertainment at a reasonable price." Cemilo also included recipes for dishes reputed to be anaphrodisiacal, scatological spells attacking Pepin the Short and his heirs, and a supposedly complete listing of home addresses for "over three hundred accommodating sprites."

Even with this farrago of false information, the *Grey Book* might have remained a period piece were it not for one extraordinary feature. Appended to one of the recipes in his "Cook's Tour of the Infernal Regions," Cemilo included the tale of one Brutto, a wheelwright who had drunk the Elixir of Life and had found the results short of the promise: like Tithonus, he finds that age without capability resembles "the hangover without the draft." This "worthy but desperate soul," so swears Cemilo, had been trying to kill himself for 151 years. The famed elixir countered all attempts: Brutto stabs himself and the knife breaks, he hangs from a tree and the rope snaps, he sets fire to his clothing and the clouds open. Ultimately he is reduced to a Bartolemeo Fair attraction, lying in front of heavily loaded ox carts to impress onlookers who marvel that he is not crushed.

By the process that critics call "creatistic fusion," the character was absorbed by his creator, and the futility of the eternal loser's life was connected in popular usage with the author: the transalpine tag "schlemihl," meaning someone who can do nothing right, is a corruption of Cemilo. German authors from Grimmelshausen on have paid homage to his contribution in demotic "Schlemihlissimus" picaresques. Werkan Zahgen of the University of Tedesco has charted this influence extensively in his *From Cheiron to Ponce de Leon: A History of the Undead*.

Proverbs of Africa (14th Century?)

"Griot Mbabo"

In 1754, the British slave trader Isaac Bristoe published a volume of proverbs he had collected, along with his human cargo, around the mouth of the Niger River. West African culture having not yet attained a European market value, nobody paid it any notice, and the book was remaindered in six months. A little over two hundred years later, during the 1960s black history revival, Ghanaian scholar Hilla Agbodeka rediscovered it, changed the title from *The*

Wit and Wisdom of the Negroe to *Proverbs of Africa*, and repub-
lished it with a preface and annotations. In the ensuing twenty
years, more than one reader has agreed with her observation that
the author, "Griot Mbabo," displayed "the wit of Aesop, the wisdom of Confucius, and the soil's own soul."

The identity of the author is uncertain. In his preface Bristoe
wrote, "The Negroes call Griot Mbabo a great teacher and give his
period as the 'days of Mansa Musa,' which I calculate as about the
time of the Conquest." Actually the great "sultan of Timbuktu"
lived in the fourteenth century—two hundred and fifty years after
Hastings—and Agbodeka cited this discrepancy as evidence of
Bristoe's Eurocentric ignorance. Further evidence, she wrote, lay
in his conviction that "Griot" and "Mbabo" were the first and
last names of his author. An African *griot* is a storyteller, entrusted with transmitting oral tradition. Mbabo is a mountain in
present-day Cameroon. Thus "Griot Mbabo," said Agbodeka, probably meant "the *griot* from near Mt. Mbabo," and could have referred to a single individual, a group of individuals, or "the Mbabo
region's oral tradition itself, as handed down by centuries of *griots*.
Assigning clear authorship to one man is senseless; it is like saying
that Percy composed his *reliques*, or that the Grimm brothers invented their *Märchen*."

Whoever wrote them, the proverbs themselves are a happy find.
By turns speculative and concrete, ingenious and blunt, expan-
sively poetic and crudely mundane, they express all the nuances
of motherwit that one associates with Aesop and Poor Richard.
Many of them have equivalents in European folklore: "You cannot
both feast and be wealthy," for example, sounds like our "You
cannot have your cake and eat it, too." But others are insistently
African in sensibility, like the *Kuchenwitz* "The iron won't get hot
if you don't put it in the fire," and the wry skewering of killjoys,
"If you cannot dance, you blame the drum." All have a freshness
of expression that recommends the book to readers of any era.

Part of that freshness, it should be said, derives from the Bristoe
transliteration—a phonetic approximation of the pidgin English in

which his captives told him their gems. For each of the 116 proverbs he attributed to Griot Mbabo, he provided both the phonetic spelling and a more conventional English "translation." Agbodeka, while regretting Bristoe's failure to transcribe the original African phrasings, admits that his management of the pidgin "pretty fairly represents the ingenuity of all Niger Basin contact tongues." (For a selection of Bristoe's "double entries," see Appendix C of this volume.)

Bodo Saved (14th Century)

The Ridgewalker Poet

Since this caustic, alliterative satire was discovered in the same Dryburgh Abbey crypt that yielded the romance *Hunt the Unicorn*, scholars long assumed it was the work of Alec of Yarrow. Because of stylistic peculiarities, this assumption is now considered unfounded, and the piece is assigned to Alec's shadowy companion, the so-called Ridgewalker Poet.

The "Boddo bokke" (as Alec calls it in the romance) is an attack on church government, or rather on its abuse by the superstitious. Bodo, a peasant, suffers from "visions"—a common enough occurrence in the fourteenth century. But unlike the visions of Langland's Piers Ploughman, for example, Bodo's are brought on by inebriation, and they have an intoxicating quality that Langland's lack. The Ridgewalker Poet makes much of the semantic links between "spirits," the "Holy Spirit," and the "Holly Spright," an impish, holly-clad apparition who torments Bodo by misquoting scripture. Convinced by the Holly Spright that "blissed barley" is a gift God intends his creatures to abuse—"For if that God hath given onlye goode/he serveth best who serveth yet a round," the imp advises—he falls ever deeper into drink, and halfway through the 1300 lines of the poem is about to drown himself to escape his misery.

At this point the action takes a bizarre turn. Saved from drowning by a wandering pardoner, he is unable to pay the man's customary indulgences fee, and is brought before an ecclesiastical court to be tried for the sin of attempted murder. When the inquiry reveals the source of his despair, he is found guilty not only of the stated charge, but also of heresy and possession, and is condemned to be executed the following day. The court decrees that he shall be drowned in the same pond in which he had failed to drown himself.

On the night before the sentence is to be carried out, Bodo experiences a cold-turkey revelation. Gazing from his cell window onto the pond, he accepts his fate and forgives his judges, understanding that like him, they, too, "drinke at dremes fontaine." Reconciled to death, he writes a poignant parting song:

> Yonder breaketh a fickel fontaine
> Like a kidde playing at a game
> Yonder waiteth a pool of numberes
> Thinges in tyme will be the same

The next morning, singing this song, Bodo meets his death merrily, confident—as he announces in a glib heretical flourish—that he will soon be face-to-face with "the fodder and the sonne and the holly sprighte."

What fourteenth-century listeners might have made of this poem is difficult to say: it manages to fuse Manichaeism, pantheism, and Arianism with the conventional Lollardry of its day, becoming in the process what Oxford medievalist Cicely Fulham-Rhodes calls "a cornucopia of offenses." Outside of Alec's romance, there is no mention of it in the historical record, and the common suspicion that the Archbishop of Canterbury ordered all copies burned is certainly a reasonable one. Details of the Ridgewalker Poet's life may never be known, but thanks to the Dryburgh find, we now have access to his highly original mind.

The Tale of Boon Companions (ca. 1390)

Gerard Gracian and Robert Chasseur

Gracian and Chasseur were novices in the Breton order of St. Stephen from 1339 until 1348, the dreadful plague year in which they experienced a folie à deux and left the cloister for the road. Donning skull masks and flower garlands, they began a fifty-year journey around Europe, singing mystical songs and administering to the stricken masses of their turbulent century what one admirer, with anachronistic acumen, called "a kind of impromptu shock therapy." The record they left of that journey is the erratic, antinomian *Tale of Boon Companions*.

For most of their half-century as wandering minstrels, Gracian and Chasseur were less musicians than forces of nature. They possessed not only an extremely finished lyrical style, but the ability to attract superb accompanists (their "boon companions") and—not least of all—what Alec of Yarrow called "the madness that passeth understanding." As a result, crowds and controversy followed them everywhere.

During the ergotism outbreaks of the 1360s, they were expelled from the Low Countries and Upper Saxony because of rumors that they had poisoned the water supply. In 1375 they were condemned by the Synod of Nantes for a professed interest in "pyramid power." And throughout their career they set the tune for the thousands of homeless, manic dancers who surfaced periodically to do the St. Vitus dance, the St. Stephen shuffle, and the *danse macabre*.

None of these details appears in *Boon Companions*. A blend of song lyrics, dance instructions, campfire tales, familial anecdotes, and antischolastic philosophy, the book is, in the frustrated words of Polish historian Oscar Halecky, "the least topical of any medieval chronicle." Indeed, it is hardly a chronicle at all, but a travel-framed pretext for sinuous meditations on everything from horticulture to the meaning of death. "There is no indication but graphological," Halecky says, "that the text is a fourteenth-century product. Its themes are, I am sorry to say, timeless."

What struck this parochial medievalist as disappointing has struck many other readers as satisfying; "they are comforting in a thrilling sort of way," writes Beryl Macomber in her *Wandering Dunces*. For, in spite of their public, skeletal personas, in spite of their involvement in the dances of death, there is absolutely no morbidity in their thinking. Their plague experience "cauterized their minds of fear," says Macomber, so that they were able to "embrace the awful reality of *vita brevis* with an intensely rooted, accepting sensuality." No doubt the "presentness" this lent their expression, their delight in what Pound called the radiance of sheer facticity, accounted for their unpopularity with the ruling classes. For their focus on the earth discredited heaven, and the vast religious structure that sold its promise.

We can only guess what Gracian and Chasseur might have been like as performers, but to judge from the lyrics in *Boon Companions*, neither they nor their audiences were typically "medieval." Their most famous lyric, *"Etoile noire,"* is a mystical improvisation on proofs of God; the beautifully crafted villanelle, *"Clapotis,"* displays an unusually modern talent for blunt paradox; and their frequent nods to their old patron Stephen and to *"Seigneur Dudon"* (a bungler of epic proportions) show that they knew how to play the fool as well as any.

In spite of its lack of historical specificity, *Boon Companions* remains a fascinating glimpse into the fourteenth-century mind. For a soberer, more factual record of the duo's lives, it is best to refer to Alec of Yarrow. His own *Hunt the Unicorn* mentions their visit to Lindisfarne in 1376 and their brief tenure as Charles VI's jesters in 1383. His memoir *Prester John's Band* covers their mutual journey through Provence in 1379; it is useful for its descriptions of "troubadour battles," or challenge songfests—two of which the trio won without entering.

Dinarzade's Revenge *(ca. 1450)*

Anonymous

In the introduction to the *Arabian Nights' Entertainments*, we learn that the narrator Scheherazade is betrothed to the misogynist sultan Shariah, who kills his wives on the morning after their wedding night to prevent their becoming unfaithful. Scheherazade escapes this fate by artful stalling: each evening, in the sultan's hearing, she tells a tale of adventure to her sister Dinarzade, and the ruler is so enchanted by her invention that after nearly three years, he calls her the "liberator of her sex" and spares her life. This supposedly "apocryphal" coda to the Eastern classic picks up the story at that point, by putting into the mouth of Dinarzade a passionate, horrific resolution. The final tale bears the Persian title "Night One Thousand and Two," but ever since Cory Meagher's 1967 translation, it has been known as "Dinarzade's Revenge."

Whoever wrote the brief, startling finale was evidently unimpressed by the sultan's magnanimity. In Meagher's admittedly free rendition, we find Dinarzade fuming at the tale's outset: "This pissant kills brides by the hundreds and saves one because she's got the gift of gab. For that we're supposed to kiss his ass? I don't care if she is my sister. If she stays with that sleaze, I'll kill her myself." And so saying, she weaves her own tale, which uses the famous characters of her sister's stories to impose a brutal justice on the "turbaned toad."

Before coming upon Scheherazade, Shariah had spent the better part of three years doing in one bride a night. The sister's revenge is also these sisters' revenge, for her story unfolds over the same period of time, with a different slaughtered newlywed each night first executing and then resuscitating the hapless monarch, so he suffers the same fate a thousand times. The wives are aided in this endeavor by the sultan's own favorite three characters—Sinbad, Aladdin, and Ali Baba—in manners that are appropriate to their own stories. For the first year, Sinbad helps the women to lure Shariah onto a magic carpet which crashes each night into the ocean. For the second year Aladdin lends him his famous lamp, which emits not a helpful djinn but a hooded demon. In the third and final year, Ali Baba dispatches him as his slave had dispatched the forty thieves—by inundating him in boiling oil.

The circularity of Shariah's torture has caused some to see Greek elements in Dinarzade's tale: Rennie Pilobolus calls it "the Persian Tantalus story, in which hubris is punished by repetition." This is a just, if anachronistic, assessment. For a more expansive, and equally anachronistic, view, see Meagher's bitterly funny introduction, in which Sappho, Dinarzade, and Valerie Solanis—author of the much-underrated *SCUM Manifesto*—are made "a triumvirate of Nike as nag, spots of lightness in a phallus-heavy world."

The Bristol Tapestry *(1491)*

Thomas Rowley

Thanks to the appropriation of his name by the eighteenth-century forger Thomas Chatterton, Rowley is generally conceded to be, in the words of the *Reader's Encyclopedia*, a "nonexistent monk, poet, and antiquarian of the fifteenth century." The disservice thus done to the real Rowley is particularly unfortunate in that it deflects attention from his masterly play cycle, *The Bristol Tapestry*. That this work bears little resemblance to the "marvellous boy's" poem *Bristowe Tragedie* enhances rather than blunts its appeal.

Rowley lived in that unstable but fertile period that Huizinga has aptly named the "waning of the Middle Ages." In Europe generally, but especially in post-Chaucerian England, popular taste in this period tended simultaneously toward the devout and the fantastic, toward the homiletic strictures of the High Middle Ages and the frothing secularity of the proto-Renaissance. One may appreciate the paradoxes that evolved from this divided sensibility by noting the three most popular literary works in the reign of Henry VII: the still vital biblical mystery plays, John Mandeville's exotic book of travels, and Malory's *Morte d'Arthur*, first printed by William Caxton in 1485.

Rowley's genius was to weave the disparate strands of liturgical drama, travelogue, and knightly romance into a single (if uneven) whole. His *Tapestry* comprises seventeen "wondere playes" addressing not only biblical matters but also such relatively arcane issues as which type of dragons breathe fire, whether the metrics of Alan à Dale are superior to those of Alec of Yarrow, and the whereabouts of the Big Rock Candy Mountain.

Famous for its reckless fusing of genres (his most famous Old Testament play was entitled *Noah and the Sea Serpent*), Rowley's creation both honored and transcended the medieval world. His traditional piety is evident in his treatment of St. Uncumber, the patroness of unhappy wives, and the so-called luncheon saint, St. Hamm of Rye. At the same time, hints of the New Learning show through in his taxonomic "monster litanies" and in his quite modern, sociological portrayal (in *Cain and His Kin*) of the Bristol pickpocket Jon Fleece. This variety, sadly, is quite obliterated in Chatterton's "accurate" but plodding rhymes.

The Quack's Repentance (1519)

Thomas of Hales

The contemporary war of nerviness between minions of medical orthodoxy and proponents of New Age tyrotechniques had an analogue in the sixteenth century, when university trained surgeons vied for favor with traditional folk healers and relic hawkers. In the biting conflict between these two camps, *The Quack's Repentance* played a significant role.

Published one year after the incorporation of the London College of Physicians, the book applauded the founding of this school as a "verry necesary Bastionne against the Falsse Depradationes of the unlerned," and condemned the "crossroads Witte" of underground healers as "unholy Dabblinge in the works of the Devil." Thus, quite apart from the fascinating glimpses it gives into Renaissance medicine, the book is invaluable as an example of professional pique and self-congratulation.

Its author was Gloucestershire's "doubting Thomas"—the same percipient and vindictive physician who in 1507 had exposed his town's most famous relic as a vial not of Christ's, but of duck's, blood. Using this scandal as an opening salvo, in *The Quack's Repentance* he recorded numerous other tales of bad faith, including those of the notorious Saxon Leecher, who used common earthworms in place of "righteousse suckers"; Thomas Pavil, who advised sipping mercury as a means of "quickening the blood"; and Dame Mary Goot of Heryon, whom Hales condemned for her notion that the introduction of chimneys caused coughing.

As this last example implies, Hales's catalog of penitent "quacks" itself often rested on shaky science. He announced his volume as a "revelation of those Ignorant Persons of whom the greatt Part have no manner of Insite," and yet in several cases, like that of Mary Goot, modern science has vindicated his villains. Thus the book is often read today—especially by advocates of "alternate medicine"—as evidence of professionalized obtuseness; the contemporary "white witch" Xenia Quarles speaks for many when she calls Hales "the prototype of the real quack, the modern, more-empirical-than-thou physician."

This may be as unfair to Hales as to his descendants. His arrogance, it is true, could be irritating, and he certainly reduces professional courtesy to absurdity when he calls France's famous surgeon Ambrose Pare "the fourth person of the Blessed Trinity." But his tone was not extreme for his age, and however tendentious it may be, his skepticism about nondegreed healers was a failing not of logic but of perspective. Quarles—for all her own tendentiousness—is quite right in saying that, had Hales turned his "acutely critical eye" on his own colleagues, "his praise of folly might have been complete." As it stands, *The Quack's Repentance* remains what it surely was even for his less "enlightened" contemporaries: a mordantly irritating survey of human error.

The Endless Journey (1523)

Guido Treno

This Renaissance science fiction tale was Treno's sprightly contribution to a heated debate over mechanization that animated Milan in the 1520s. The controversy began when the city council discovered a notebook of recently deceased favorite son Leonardo da Vinci, containing his plans for an automated trolley system to be run by steam power, vast pulleys, and spiral springs. Council technocrats, who had been frustrated for years in their attempts to develop the master's flying machines, saw the trolley system as a benign alternative and a means of easing mechanization into public favor. Their opponents, citing expense, noise, and danger, condemned the projected system as "a satanic engine," and vowed to keep it off the streets at all costs.

Treno owned a sedan chair company, and since his business stood to suffer from the project, he soon became point man for the opposition. His attack on technology included a string of vitriolic public speeches that have been forgotten and one monitory fable that brought him fame. In *Il viaggio senza fine*, which remained popular in antiscientific circles into the eighteenth century, Treno told the tale of the chandler Carlo, who one morning in 1525 becomes the first passenger on the newly installed trolley system. The honor soon proves to be a curse, for the braking system has been inexpertly put together, and the cars never come to a complete stop: as a result, Carlo cannot disembark, and seems condemned to be "the first, and eternal victim" of the Milano Transportatione Automattica.

Faced with this affront to their ingenuity, the city fathers call a special meeting to assess whether the luckless experience of one timid passenger dictates shutting down the marvel altogether—at least long enough to inspect the brakes. As they debate, however, the city plunges gradually into darkness, since Carlo is no ordinary chandler: he has been chosen as the first rider, in fact, because his candles supply eighty percent of the city's lighting. Faced with this conundrum, the council halts the device, and Carlo is set back on solid ground.

Unfortunately, the experience has so disoriented him that he vows never to make another candle. He retires first to a Calabrian monastery and then, unable to regain his composure even in this immutable environment, to an asylum for the "permanently confused" located in the south of London. He thus begins the long Mediterranean tradition of expatriated schizophrenia.

Treno's story turned the tide against the technocrats, and the trolley system that he warned against was not built until Mussolini's time. Even then, nostalgia for the pre-industrial era was so strong that, as an ironic gesture in Treno's direction, the Milan subway authority adopted as its motto Carlo's parting shot to his native town: *"Troppo veloce per me, mille grazie."*

The Unbook Book *(1530s?)*

Victor Boulemerd

In the second book of *Gargantua and Pantagruel*, Rabelais gives us a catalog of books from the library of the St. Victor Abbey—a famous Paris center of theological learning. Typically scatological and erudite, it mocks the pretensions of scholasticism by vulgarizing the most abstruse concepts in titles like "Greek Prepositions Discussed by the Turdicants" and "The Ape's Paternoster."

Until recently, this catalog was taken as a typical Rabelaisian joke: a satire framed in an elaborate conceit. The 1967 discovery of the famous "oval office" in the Sorbonne, however, identified another author and a wider meaning.

As is now widely known, the secret oval room in the university's crypt was revealed during the riotous *"événements du mai,"* when a wayward cobblestone broke the hidden latch that had kept its door closed for four hundred years. Inside were a cot, a writing table, several quills, an inkstand—and a manuscript entitled *Biblia Abiblia*, which instantly transformed Rabelaisian scholarship. Written in a meticulous, Florentine script by a monk known only as Fra Boulemerd, it contained what were evidently the complete texts of the 139 volumes in Rabelais's catalog, from *Bigua Salutis* (The Props of Salvation) to Merlin Coccaius's *De Patria Diabolorum* (On the Country of the Devils).

Most of the texts in this collection are only a few pages long—more planning sketches than completed works. "The Prelate's Bagpipe," for example, covers only two sides of a single parchment, and "Father Gobble's" essay on bacon eating, which Rabelais has in three volumes, is in toto only three thousand words. In spite of their brevity, however, Boulemerd's texts constitute a significant find, for the monk was as learned as Rabelais himself, and his manuscript is a cornucopia of fascinating trivia. In texts like "Mayr's Pudding Making" and "Bricot's Varieties of Soups," we have invaluable glosses on Renaissance cookery. In such satires as "The Shitter's Martingale" and "The Bellows of the Alchemists," we find scatology refined into revelation. And in theological works like "The Scrawlings of Scotus" and "The Geography of Purgatory," we find at work a mind (as Bombastus has it) "as subtile as zephyred gossamer, yet taut as Cain." It is with justice that Boulemerd dubs himself, on the title page, *"l'éponge du cabinet ovale,"* or the "sponge of the oval office."

Half in French and half in Latin, the manuscript was first translated by Constance Chimera in 1969 as *The Unbook Book*. A second translation, now under way, will include translator Claude Pluvier's speculations on the relationship between Fra Boulemerd and Rabelais—which to this day is unexplained.

The Art of Giving Offense *(1532)*

Girolamo Vitelloni

Denied a preferment by the Duke of Urbino in 1531, the Mantuan nobleman Vitelloni took revenge by publishing a flip, acerbic "companion volume" to Baldassar Castiglione's *Il cortegiano*, which the duke had both sponsored and promoted. Castiglione's famous volume had detailed the necessary attributes of the *uomo universale*, including a perfect familiarity with courtly etiquette. Vitelloni mocked the very idea of etiquette, not only in his "snapshot potshots at Urbino's hotshots" (in Toccata's inelegant translation of Burkhardt), but also in his close instructions for giving offense. The bulk of his *Manuale maschio*—translated in 1537 as *The Manly Arte of Giving Offense*—was a string of detailed guidelines for insulting rivals.

Sixteenth-century Italy was no stranger to the "point of honor," and Vitelloni got great mileage out of his countrymen's testiness. He listed nearly three hundred *verbi offensivi* which, he assured his readers, any "true man" (*uomo reale*) would take as incitement to a duel. In his catalog of *gesti offensivi*, he invented derisive gestures that survive today in such expressions as "back of one's hand" and "laughing up one's sleeve." And, in an elaborately framed philosophical discourse on *atti offensivi*, he laid the groundwork for the seventeenth-century fad of employing practical jokes in social climbing: among the most popular of these jokes was the muddying of a rival's coat of arms, a practice that gave us the expression "name of mud."

The twitted duke was not amused with this effrontery. He banished Vitelloni in 1536, in what he archly announced as a measure "protective of public morality." The satirist made his way to England, where he aided another disgruntled sinecure seeker, William Foxpaw, in making a 1537 translation. For a time his boorish divertissement became as voguish across the Channel as it had been in his native land, and a Vitelloni Society, based in Brackwater, spread the gospel of outrageous behavior as a needed foil to courtly pretensions. Henry VII, originally charmed by its members' excesses, turned against them in 1539 when they advised burning the toasts used to drink the king's health as a reminder that "even Monarches turne to assh." Condemned by royal edict, the young sparks dispersed and the society died.

The odd writer's fate in the modern world has been only marginally better. Coarse practical joking enjoyed a brief revival in Rome after the showing of Federico Fellini's laudatory memoir *I Vitelloni* (1958), but for the most part his sensibility has proved too abrasive for the era of fern bars and famine. He has become, at least for this generation, what Castiglione called his Gaspar Pallavicino: a "somewhat shifty disputant."

The Helper's Helper (1563)

Heloise Hausenhintsen

This book is thought to be the Western world's first textbook of home economics or, as it was known in the seventeenth and eighteenth centuries, "household management." A series of "step-by-step lessons" on *"matières domestiques,"* it advises servants and servants-to-be on roast temperatures, spot removal, bed making, antimacassar arrangement, crumber usage, and a host of other particulars essential to the running of a "quality" household.

Published privately in Geneva, this catalog of tips to domestics enjoyed a popularity beyond its intended audience largely because it was interpreted as a "code" book twitting the excesses and pretensions of Calvin's theocracy. The sense of religious in-joking—

to those who had their eyes peeled for double meanings—seemed particularly strong, and was explained in various "decoding manuals" that followed the book's publication. In one of these, for example, the author interprets Heloise's suggestion that mutton be accompanied by red wine as "the popish counsel that the flock of Christ may be saved but by the blood of Rome." The lengthy discussion of starched collar styles was seen as an attack on the vanity of magistrates, and the equally detailed "guidelines for needle threading" were seen as snaps at the Calvinist proclivity for equating worldly riches with election. To nervous Calvinists, this kind of thing smacked of blasphemy, and the volume was censored in 1546, only to enjoy an even wider reputation underground.

Hausenhintsen's manual has survived longer than such competitors as Ringer's *The Well-made Bed* and Bern's *Miladies Toylette Bettered* because of an entrepreneurial accident. In 1603, as financier Konradin Echtergrinzen was laying the foundations of the Swiss hotel industry, he came upon a copy of *Der Hilfershilfer* which so captivated his imagination that he made it required reading for all his staff. An Urritz Hotel servant's copy, left inadvertently in an English guest's room, opened a British market, and by the middle of the seventeenth century, "Dame Heloise" was as popular in London as in Geneva.

The author herself consistently denied that the book had any but a surface import, and it is certainly possible to read her information straight, as training material for a growing servant class. Whatever theory one prefers, the book remains a storehouse of Renaissance trivia on the domestic arts, as well as a fair guide to folk beliefs. The popularity of the flower edelweiss as an anaphrodisiac, for example, may be directly traced to Hausenhintsen's volume; and a common Swiss method of removing salt from a tablecloth—dribbling wine upon the spill—is also a Frau Heloise invention.

The book remains useful today. Indeed, in several of the Alpine country's cantons, brides are traditionally presented with the book as part of their *paquets nuptiaux*. That the volume has become a *vade mecum* for *hausfrauen* would no doubt have astounded the woman who meant it as a guide to their help. In her own caustic admonition, "No true lady ever did laundry."

Boggle's Counsel *(1581)*

Iago Hamm(?)

To Elizabethans, Boggle was a kind of urban Puck: a goodhearted but troublesome jokester who got the credit for any mischief of unclear origin. Christopher Headwell's 1569 farce *Hieronimo's Madd Again*, building on a folklore tradition, calls him "that smiling breaker of caskets and oaths." The London City Council in 1573, displaying a certain puckishness of its own, issued an official investigative finding citing "one Master Boggle of the boroughe of Kensingeton" as the probable culprit in a series of sewage-pipe ruptures. It was Boggle to whom Shakespeare was referring when, in the second act of *Hamletta*, Polonius responds to Ophelia's "strangeness" by saying, "It confuseth, it confoundeth, it bewildereth, it tendeth to redendancie, it boggleth the minde."

Boggle's Book lays out conventional wisdom as it might be rephrased by this celebrated minx. Not the Heywoodism "Haste maketh waste" but "Haste maketh the meeting on time." Not "A bird in the hand weigheth more than a pair in the bush" but "A bird in hande pecketh at ye wriste." Not "hitting the naile upon the head" but "hitting Nyall upon the head" (William Nyall being the queen's whipping boy). And so on through hundreds of other maxims, so that the compendium at large fulfilled its promise of offering wisdom "as seen through a darke, gassily."

For three years, the self-proclaimed "gentil travestie" enjoyed a vogue in London and beyond. But when the anonymous author included several "inflammatory" proverbs in an expanded 1584 edition, it was banned as "an insulte to Her Majestie." (Specifically, "Politics makes strange bedfellows, but poetry stranger" was seen as a reference to the open secret that Elizabeth and Walter Raleigh had been lovers.) The queen herself issued an order for the "discoverie and arrest of the miscreante," but the ensuing investigation proved inconclusive: no "certaine culprit" could be found, and the authorship remains in doubt to this day.

The folio edition, entitled *Boggles Boke of Wise Counselle for Sundrie Occasions*, bore only the initials "I.H." Because many of the parodied maxims had appeared in John Heywood's popular 1562 collection *Proverbs*, many readers suspected him as the author, and took the book as an allusion to his own success. The erudition of the 1581 volume supports that belief, but Heywood himself vigorously denied it, and recent vowel-weighting comparisons of the two texts suggest he was not merely protecting his skin. "The preponderance of long *e* alone in penultimate position," argues Geoffrey Gudge of the Cambridge Doremist Society, "points unswervingly toward the figure of Iago Hamm."

Born Hammo in Milan, Iago Hamm was a minor poet and major adventurer who left his homeland in the 1560s to serve first in the Spanish, then the Dutch, and finally the English navy before settling in Canterbury in 1571. There he vowed to devote himself to poetry and prayer and "to write the unrecorded history of my race." The first installment of that history was a dreadful sonnet cycle, *The Spanish Main* (1573), in which privateering is made a mode of contemplation. The second was the equally dreary *Meditatione upone Digitts* (1576), an elaborate social history of thumb wrestling. If Hamm was indeed the author of *Boggle's Book*, the compendium was his third effort. For the definitive statement of that position, see Gudge's chapter "The Milanesian Connection" in his just-reprinted *Beyond the Joy of Lex*.

The Demon Count (1582)

Jean Weir and Gaspar Fromenteau

In the latter half of the sixteenth century, to meet the accounting needs of a rapidly expanding merchant class, mathematicians dedicated themselves to improving notational systems, thus facilitating the ledger management of growing fortunes. Two of the enduring legacies of this period were Simon Stevin's introduction of decimal fractions and Robert Napier's invention of a primitive calculator—the multiplier-effect device called "Napier's bones." One of the lesser known but equally fascinating achievements was the "demon count" project of Weir and Fromenteau.

Flemish-born Weir was court physician to the Duke of Cleves, a backwater potentate whose hold on his era's pragmatic spirit was so tenuous that in 1580 he commanded Weir to produce a "definitive accounting of the planet's demon population," to be used both as a data bank and a pharmacological reference. The duke's scheme was to match up each demon with a disease, a *"recette sanitaire,"* and a prophylactic prayer. He did not live to see that scheme completed, but he did get to see his doctor's catalog.

According to Weir's calculations, the planet was infested with 7,409,127 demons, under the command of seventy-nine princes. This allowed for 93,786 demons to each prince, with the remaining 33 forming a specialized "mischief unit" (responsible for breaking glasses, causing hiccups, and the like) which Weir called the *compagnie des vauriens*, or "scamp covey"—generally misconstrued by English typesetters as "scamp coven." These findings were most gratifying to the duke, who had long suspected that the traditional belief in over one billion demons was ill founded.

But Weir's scholarship was not universally approved. In 1581, after having worked out his own figure for the demon horde, the Rouen bank examiner Fromenteau denounced Weir in a famous broadside as insincere. His "count," said the Frenchman, was a hoax, designed to placate a dotty patron and win him fame. The actual figure was over 3000 demons less: 7,405,926. This product of the Great Pythagorean Number (1234321) and the number of earthly continents (6)* represented, in Fromenteau's modest analysis, "a reservoir of malice quite sufficient for the appropriate torment of humanity."

Weir responded to the banker's charge in a vitriolic attack on the New Mathematics, and this ushered in a public exchange of vilification which fascinated readers upon its appearance in book form in 1619, and which even today has lost little of its appeal. The book's aroma of high dudgeon is enhanced by frequent obiter dicta regarding contemporary events, and even those who find pre-Cartesian dialectics arcane can hardly fail to be enchanted by Weir's analogies between demon counting and household tasks, or Fromenteau's aphoristic dismissals of "famous frauds." The best-known of his quips still resonate today: his slap at Napier as the *homme au os*, or "man of the bone," gave us "boner" and "uh-oh" to indicate failure; and his epithet for Weir himself, *Le Gaufrier Belgique*, translates as our "Belgian waffler."

The Dream of Night (1584)

Joanna the Mad

During Spain's *siglio d'oro*, the monastic Carmelite order produced three writers of genius: Teresa of Avila, John of the Cross, and Joanna the Mad. The mystical eloquence of the first two was acknowledged in their own lifetimes, and the Church, not long after their deaths, paid them the honor of making them saints. Not so

---

* Australia, of course, had not yet been discovered. What Fromenteau had in mind was Europe, Asia, Africa, the two Americas, and Greenland. The question of why uninhabited Greenland needed any demons at all Fromenteau tackled in a prophetic chapter entitled "Beyond Armageddon: God's Blueprint for Urban Renewal."

with Juana la Loca. Her long poem *El sueño de la noche* is equal in imagery and religious intelligence to anything in Teresa or John; yet she was neglected, and even abused, in her time—and still awaits canonization today.

The reason, quite clearly, was political—or, to be more precise, patriarchal. For Joanna was as enthusiastic about "worldly" learning as she was about matters of the spirit. She was fascinated particularly by science, and she filled notebooks with observations about nature. To the sixteenth-century Church fathers, such interests would have been suspect in a layperson; they were definitely unseemly in a nun, and as a result Joanna had to contend constantly with the disapproval, and eventually censure, of her superiors. A 1587 reprimand by a Zaragozan bishop, counseling her, in effect, to behave more like a woman, prompted a defense of her inquiries, *La respuesta* (The Response), which has been called "one of the great works of feminism." But it did her little good at the time. Publicly vilified as disobedient, she acquired a sobriquet that had belonged to Queen Joanna of Castile fifty years earlier, and even her fervent and quite unworldly poetry lost the sanction of her parish.

El sueño could not be directly condemned, even by as regressive an institution as the Spanish church, for its intense piety was unmistakable, and before her stubbornness it had already been highly praised by the very priests who denounced *La respuesta*. As a religious meditation, it explores the same "soul's darkness" that John had explored some years earlier, but it does so with a verbal ingenuity that prefigures the Metaphysicals by a generation. The triple ambiguity of the title, moreover—is the poet dreaming at night, or of the night, or is the night itself dreaming?—lends the work a sense of thoughtful tension that is beautifully replicated in its conceits. No wonder it inspired Calderon de la Barca to write his own secular meditation *La vida es sueño*. Or that Borges, in his *Historia universal de la infamia*, called the rediscovery in the 1920s of *"la loca muy sana"* "the night's awakening from its dream that the dream itself was asleep."

One final irony in Joanna's story: A century after her death, another Carmelite nun, also named Juana, became the most celebrated poet in Spanish Mexico with a series of quatrains about love. This second Juana—her monastic name was Juana de la Cruz—also wrote a poem called *El sueño*, and was reprimanded for a treatise called *La respuesta*. Because the paired texts are similar in theme and style, the two women are frequently confused. For an investigation of this strange coincidence, see Ines de Abasje y Ramirez, "The Two Juanas: A Study in Retroactive Influence," in the June 1942 *Revista Castiliana*.

Hamletta (ca. 1589)

William Shakespeare

Scholars have known for centuries that the Bard of Avon wrote two Hamlet plays: the version that everyone knows, first produced in 1601, and an earlier, lost version from about 1589, usually referred to as the "Ur-Hamlet." In a recent housecleaning at the Bodleian Library, a manuscript was discovered that many Shakespeareans are convinced is the long-hidden original play.

In terms of imagery, poetics, depth of characterization—all the elements of dramaturgy in which Shakespeare excelled—the Bodleian manuscript is pedestrian: the shaky product of a twenty-five-year-old poet who had not yet found his voice or his theme. Its plot, however, is remarkable, for here the prince's celebrated reflectiveness has little to do with the murder of his father, and much to do with the fact that "he" is a girl.

Princess Hamletta, in this play, dons male clothing for self-protection. Her mother and father, the king and queen, are, she believes, plotting to kill her to keep her from inheriting the throne; to foil them, she disappears while on a hunting party, spreads the rumor she has been devoured by doves, and returns incognito as her cousin Winchell, a dotty ne'er-do-well who threatens no one. Her speeches as Winchell are stand-up comedy, and indeed the play as a whole is hardly tragic. The murder plot proves to be a figment of the princess's overactive imagination: she has misinterpreted her parents' boudoir murmurings that they love her so much they could "eat her up." And the bloody dénouement of the 1601 play appears here in much lighter form: the final battle is a palace-wide food fight.

As M. Breckenridge points out in her study *Elizabethan Cross-Dressers*, transvestism was common in Renaissance drama because women generally did not act. Indeed, the Bard of Avon himself got his start by playing girls' roles on London stages. It has been suggested that he meant *Hamletta* as adolescent revenge, mocking the stage conventions through inversion; certainly there is bite in the princess's observation that "such fripperies do not a lass become/so much as a draped cow doth hide her milk"—and a rich, multivalent irony in the fact that in an Elizabethan production, Hamletta would have been a male playing a female playing a male.

Curiously enough, the "cross-dressed *Hamlet*" that has taken the English-speaking world by surprise has been known to the Danes for many years. In Danish folklore, Hamletta is a popular heroine who twits the vanity of the self-important by "playing at queen." She was portrayed on the silent screen in 1920 by the legendary Danish actress Asta Nielsen. The film's director, incidentally, was Sven Gade—the real-life model for the "Hungarian" hypnotist Svengali.

The Flute Thief *(ca. 1600)*

Anonymous

One of the unsolved puzzles of North American archaeology is the abrupt disappearance of the Anasazi. From about the time of the fall of Rome to the late twelfth century, these enterprising agricultural people inhabited what is now known as the Four Corners of the American southwest, around the intersection of Colorado, Utah, Arizona, and New Mexico. There they built vast adobe apartment complexes that the Spanish called pueblos, created magnificent pottery, and with the use of gravitational irrigation made the desert bloom. Then, quite suddenly around the year 1300, they were gone, obliterated from the archaeological record almost overnight by unexplained forces.

Citing tree rings as evidence, most archaeologists identify drought as the culprit. A more esoteric explanation is to be found in *The Flute Thief* (also known as the Mesa Verde Codex), discovered a century ago in the Franciscan mission of San Josef Piscopo, just north of San Bernardino. Written in a unique blend of doggerel Spanish and literary Athabaskan, it tells the tale of an Anasazi girl named Chingara who steals the young men's sacred flute bundle and, by sacrilegiously playing the "male only" instruments, destroys her entire culture.

The problem created by the theft is not simply the fracture of traditional gender roles. It is that the girl plays so sweetly that her listeners in effect forget to live—or rather, forget to perform the necessary functions of survival in their arid environment. Captivated by her melodies, men "put their rabbit sticks away and leave the hunting to the coyotes"; women lay down their dibble sticks and "trust the Corn Mother to plant the ears herself"; children forget to attend the spring initiation ceremonies; and the high priest neglects the sacrifices essential for the annual ceremonial Gila Roast. Eventually the people stop cooking, eating, and—inevitably—breathing. Within weeks the population withers to anorexic proportions and then, in what the Codex calls "one far-off divine event to which the whole creation moves," is assumed en masse into heaven: transported beyond bodily process by listening to Chingara's playing, the People of the Rock are transformed into the People of the Air.

No one really knows who wrote this "modern myth," or for what purpose. In southwestern historiography, it has always been an occult curiosity, applauded by those who find its ascetic elements ennobling, vilified by those who see it, in the words of Rosinante Castañada, as "the quintessential masochist's whine, a vicious public endorsement of autogenocide." Current scholarship takes a less psychological approach, seeing Chingara as symbolic of ecological change; it can hardly be accidental, Royal Broadfoot points out, that *ch'iin kan dra* in Athabaskan means "It has not rained."

Chingara's influence continues to be felt in North American culture. Some see her as a kind of ZPG goddess, with descendants in the self-abnegating Shakers. To the more traditional-minded people of the Four Corners today, she is the originator of the Snake Flute cult dances. There is even a contemporary millennialist belief that when Chingara plays her stolen flutes again, the Anasazi will return to rule a "purified" planet.

The London Diary *(1617)*

Rebecca Rolfe (Pocahontas)

There are few Americans alive who do not know the tale of Pocahontas, the teenage daughter of Powhatan who, when Captain John Smith was about to be brained to death by her people, threw her body across his and saved his life. For most people, the tale stops there, or drifts off into romantic hyperbole, with the Indian girl and the soldier getting married. Pocahontas did not marry Smith, but a tobacco farmer by the name of John Rolfe; baptised Rebecca, Mrs. Rolfe bore her husband a son and in 1616 accompanied him to England.

The English loved her. Jacobean London had an avid taste for novelty—witness the "Pulcinella scare" of 1612, or the social frenzy generated by Rolfe's tobacco—and they took to the Indian princess like a courtier to snuff. King James himself granted her an audience. In her honor pubs were renamed *"La Belle Sauvage"* and "The Princess." Delighted that she had graced a performance of his masque *The Vision of Delight*, Ben Jonson wrote a poem for her (see Appendix D). Duded up in the latest London styles and speaking what Smith called "such English as might well bee understood," the Lady Rebecca was the nine days' wonder of her time.

To hear the English tell it, it was her freshness and simplicity that turned them on. "Like unto not a Rose but a Bouquet of wilde Thyme woulde I calle thys winsomme Childe," observed Jonson's friend Rhett Boddeler upon meeting her. "If lasses there had beyn in Edene, mighte shee have beyn theyre Nonpareil." The subject's own view of the matter was less sublime, as her English diary makes clear. According to Pocahontas, her London hosts viewed her with a discomfiting blend of salaciousness, racism, and hauteur. More than once her pen records "shamefull congresses" in which young sparks—embracing the stereotype of Indian lubricity—"sang sweetly to me above theyre starchedde collares, the while theyre handes mayde different observationes." And even those Londoners who managed to comport themselves "as theye tell mee a gentillmann shud" seemed prone to boorish intrusions. The girl's diary entry for January 12, 1617, makes the sad point well:

> To the verry Christian subjects of theyre magesties pleasure I seeme not a fellowe but a suspect personne. Theye list not that orlorde Gesus hears mye prayers as hee heares those of longer communicationes. I am in theyre congregationes a seconde class worshipper and this bee true no lesse at dance or table. It is a wonderment to somany that I forke mye foode, and an amusement to them whan I shud dance, so that milord Rolfe hath forbade mee dancing, that I ceese to bee theyre monkey on a stringe.

Pocahontas's diary, covering the period between her arrival in England in June of 1616 and her death from smallpox nine months later, grows increasingly depressing in tone as the young princess becomes more disillusioned at the "fancee fixe" she has gotten herself into. Yet its lugubriousness is frequently balanced by what the writer herself calls her "bubblinge algonkwin gaiety," so that the ultimate sense of the volume is encouraging. Rex Thattagill goes so far as to proclaim it "a triumph of native spirit over ortho-doxy" as well as "the first anti-Bildungsroman on the American continent."

Stairway to Heaven (1618)

Jorge Jerez de la Frontera

The most famous dramatic productions of Spain's Golden Age—the plays and *autos sacramentales* of Calderón and Lope de Vega—were viewed by large audiences in their own time, and are rightly accounted masterpieces of popular theater. The smaller court plays known as *autos efemerales*, or simply *efemerada*, were written mostly by court functionaries, viewed only by the Castilian inner court, and forgotten almost as soon as they went on. They are of concern today only to scholars. Yet to judge from the few that survive, they often reached heights of dramatic fervor to which El Fenix himself might have aspired.

Of the court scribblers who turned out these neglected gems, Jerez was certainly the most accomplished, and his masterpiece, *La escalera a cielo*, is as moving an evocation of Golden Age vanities as can be found anywhere in the accepted canon. Its hero, the aging Don Amadeo, wants to construct an "infinite staircase" before he dies, "to the glory of our beloved monarch and of God." This patently impossible project invites ridicule, yet Amadeo persists, first with the aid of his fellow hidalgos, then with that of his daughter Imelda, and finally—when the girl marries a sailor bound for El Dorado—alone. Because the play highlights the contrast between the single-minded devotion of the old man and the frivolity of his sunshine friends, it can be read as a satire on courtly behavior. But it also displays religious impulses, which have moved Jerez's best critic, Lucinda Jiménez-Thorne, to call *Stairway to Heaven* "the prototype of drama as prayer."

Not all viewers have been as kind. At an *efemerada* festival in Madrid in 1959, the play was shut down after two performances because Franco's minister of cultural affairs found the twitting of hidalgo etiquette to be an attack on the "*principio de la autoridad.*" Religious fundamentalists, too, have questioned its value, seeing the stairway as a modern Tower of Babel and Amadeo as God's challenger rather than servant. Both suggestions would have astounded Jerez: like Lope and Calderón, he had been ordained, and there is absolutely no question about his piety. "Calling Jerez a heretic," Jiménez-Thorne once wrote to the *Hispanic Times*, "is like calling J. Edgar Hoover an anarchist."

Even if Jerez's work had been as pedestrian as most *efemerada*, he would still deserve a place in cultural history because, although *Stairway to Heaven* was produced only once in his lifetime (his own 1619 production), a dramatic technique employed in that performance quickly spilled from the stage into Spanish life. The youngest daughter of Philip III suffered as a child from a lisp. Out of respect for the princess, then eighteen, Jerez had all his characters reproduce her affliction, so that *palacio*, for example, was spoken in the play as *palathio*. The king, charmed by the playwright's homage, adopted the affectation himself; the court and then the common people followed suit; and the so-called Castilian *c* was born.

Cacophony of the Spheres *(1651)*

Guy-Martine Ratatouille

The premise of this dramatic curiosity is that the planets, anciently named for Mediterranean deities, are indeed divinities masquerading as hunks of rock—and that they are miffed at the New Science, which consigns them to the status of harpies and chimera. A dedicated fence straddler in the "Ancients versus Moderns" con-

troversy, Ratatouille presented his play as a reification of the debate, showing that even on the celestial plane consensus was a rare commodity.

In the play, first acted at the Théâtre du Chat Qui Pêche as a prelude to Corneille's *Pertharite*, the heavenly spheres stage an extended debate to determine which of them shall destroy the earth. Participants are the sun, the moon, and the five known extraterrestrial planets. Each argues its case with mock casuistry and a deferential nod to classical tradition, and much of Ratatouille's humor comes from his skewering of legal and academic pomposity.

As the play opens, the sun is banished from the proceedings because he has become "insufferable since Copernicus made him king." With the sun gone, the moon makes her case: Since she has succeeded for centuries in deluding mortals that she is in fact a chunk of Camembert, she should be permitted to finish them off. "I will moon them, thus distracted, to extinction," she boasts. Mars and Venus counter this claim, suggesting that together they should visit the earth with "amorous frenzy" so that the "silk-draped simians" will drown in passion. Saturn objects that dying for love is too mundane a capitulation for the "bloated rabble." As governor of *la belle Arte*, he will "confound them with wonder," visiting upon them a universal case of "artist's block" so that, aesthetically thwarted, they commit mass suicide.

Finally the stage passes to giant Jupiter, whom Ratatouille nicknames *Gros Pataud* (Hulk), and flitting Mercury, whom he calls *Feu de Paille* (Flash in the Pan). The Hulk proposes that he "roll over the mighty mites as a cannonball rolls through a field of ants." Flash offers the more delicate but nonetheless lethal suggestion that he "float like a butterfly and sting like a bee," zipping around the planet at such speed that the resulting tornadoes "make of their monuments but dust in the wind."

Of this debate, nothing comes. The celestial bodies are so intent on vying with each other that, unable to come to a consensus or elect a "delegate of destruction," they opt in the end for the status quo. Thus the earth is saved by indecision, and in a queer, indirect fashion, the value of the Copernican model is vindicated, since the play ends with the planets regrouping around the duly chastised sun, accepting the presence of "testy, tumid Terra" as a necessary evil in the cosmic design.

Whether Ratatouille meant this dénouement as "proof" of the Polish astronomer's mathematical model, or as a snappish critique of countervailing professorial orthodoxies (the Mannheim versus the Lyon school, for example) has never been firmly ascertained. Whatever his intent, the play does function as a uniquely fanciful comment on the New Learning.

The Tripe Master *(1666)*

Gustave de La Procope

Procope was a gourmandizing restaurateur in Molière's day and a frequent after-show host to the theater crowd: La Procope, which still exists in Paris's French Quarter, was Sardi's to the age of snuff and *gloire*. So one might expect Procope's *livre de cuisine* to be a collection of bon mots and exotic tastes. Not so. *"Le divine Gustave"* was unusually philosophic, even for a Frenchman, and his volume treats eating as a contemplative activity. To call *Le Maître des Tripes* merely a chatty recipe book would be like calling Isaak Walton's classic *Compleat Angler* a guide to trout streams.

Tripe, of course, is cow stomachs—a delicacy in the seventeenth century no less than now, but one that enjoyed only a limited esteem because it had the reputation of being "peasant fare." In spite of this derogation—or because of it—chefs have always seen the meat as a challenge: "an empty canvas," as one put it, "which beckons genius." Thus, on a purely culinary level, this banal food summons and rewards ingenuity; and that ingenuity is surely demonstrated in this volume. Several of the recipes in Procope's book—I mention only *tripes etouffées avec les truffes* and the indescribable *tripes glacées à la manière de Tartuffe*—have become justifiable classics in their own right.

But there is much more to the book than tasty stomachs. Procope's true ingenuity lay in his presentation of tripe as "basic matter," or what Descartes would have called *res materia*, and his depiction of cuisine as a mode of thinking that aimed to "transmute" this basic matter into abstract form. Procope called this aim "the hidden dream of all of Plato's children," and he proposed his work as a "book of alchemy, where one transforms guts into gold." Molière's friend Gils Fleury acutely pointed out that in his restaurant Procope featured tripe at every meal "precisely because of its essential baseness." "If one could delight in the quidditas of this foul substance, then the buffetings of any fortune might prove bearable; they might go down as smoothly as *marron glacé*."

Whether or not Procope succeeded in his philosophical quest is of course open to interpretation. But even those who find his "kitchen idealism" wearisome see his earnest, detailed expositions as quite enchanting: "It is difficult to despise a man," admitted Fleury, "who speaks of mushrooms as if they were favored pets." And, of course, simply as a cookbook, the work is a trove of possibilities. In Yugoslavia, where tripe is even more popular than in France, Procope is a minor culture hero; in the words of Split restaurateur Bogdan Jurisic, "The man could get more out of a bag of guts than most of us can do with filet mignon."

Pair of Dice Lost (1671)

Jeremy Ludlow

John Milton's great poem *Paradise Lost* covers the biblical ground from the revolt of the rebel angels to the expulsion of Adam and Eve from Eden. Milton's younger contemporary Ludlow, who was "enthralled by Mr. Milton's sonorities," nevertheless felt the epic lacked something, and he endeavored to provide it in a "predendum." What was lacking, he felt, was a fuller depiction of Heaven *before* the revolt, when Lucifer was still the Son of Light and the favorite of God's admiring legions. "It was Mr. Milton's own picture of the Archfiend," he explained, "that compelled me to intrude myself into his poem: for I felt that a Being so fully tortured must speak his case with the *lacrimae doloris sui*, and not the bombast of a Drunkard caught out at tippling."

Ludlow was not the first or the last to question the rhetorical excesses of Milton's "Archfiend," though he was certainly unique in his response. *Pair of Dice Lost* describes the "halcyon aeons" from the beginning of Creation to Satan's defection, during which the Creator and his luminous companions amuse themselves by running interplanetary races (Satan has the record for the Mercury-to-Jupiter circuit), quaffing an ethereal beverage called "nebula," and when they tire of these exertions, gambling. Using polyfaceted "cosmic" dice, they play not for gain but for preeminence: the winners get to oversee the Milky Way for the next millennia, or (an even more coveted prize) to sit closer to God's throne.

All goes well in this celestial entertainment palace until, around nineteen aeons A.C., Satan comes to a disturbing realization: since God is both omniscient and omnipotent, there is no assurance He is not cheating at the game, either by placing his bets on a foreseeable outcome or by manipulating the dice as they fall. The favorite angel broaches this sticky subject, and is informed magisterially, "Have you then invented Morality, my shining One? And when I breathed upon the waters, where were you?"

Understandably upset at this response, Satan muses darkly, "If the Almighty will not then set down Rules, why his loyal subjects must need set down their Own." So thinking, he steals the cosmic dice, hurls them cavalierly in the direction of the planet Earth, and waits for judgment. It is not long in coming. Unable to tease an apology out of Satan for "rashly picking up My marbles and going home," God banishes him from the celestial presence and condemns him to an eternity below on Earth. "On thy belly thou must goe," Ludlow echoes Milton, "and eat dirt with the creatures that I send you; so much thou must endure until thou save my dice, and restore them to their proper home."

Satan never does find the dice—which is why, in Ludlow's wry estimation, "This green yet besieged orb of mud and mistiness/ spins yet uncertain, the Almighty's plan defied." The Latitudinarian implications of this comment won Ludlow no friends among the Puritan hierarchy, and indeed his "spirited despatch" was soon made anathema both by Canterbury and (redundantly) by Rome. In the bitter whimsy of its theme—his hint that God himself may be out of control—it speaks more strongly to the modern temper than to Ludlow's own.

The Ill-Tempered Clavier (1674)

Heinrich Walther Stichprober

This intricate mystical novel has generally been assigned footnote status in the history of Western culture. It is the book that J. S. Bach humorously acknowledged as the origin of his *Well-Tempered Clavier*, and few musicologists have ever bothered to go further than that. Assuming the work to be important only as inspiration for the master, they have tacitly concurred with Bach's own estimation of it as a *Junglingestivolispiel*, or "bagatelle for a youngster."

Actually, *Das Schlimmtemperierte Klavier* was a great deal more than that. With an empathy for human suffering that has been likened to that of Proust and Erma Bombeck, and with an eye for significant detail that matched that of his contemporary Grimmelshausen, Stichprober told the tale of Hans Castorp, a circuit-riding klavier tuner whose work symbolizes the human condition. As he goes from one German court to another, trying to keep dozens of keyboards in tune simultaneously, he becomes an archetypal Sisyphean hero, fighting against the inevitable string stretching with the same valor and existential grimness that the Greek figure summoned against gravity. As he meticulously regulates each individual instrument, bucking the subtle fluidities of contiguous strings, his task becomes reverently empirical—"a final plumbing of the Cartesian well," as Zaza Kirkel once put it. And as he strives for the *höchste Oberton*, or "ultimate harmonic," we see him as a musical mystic who uses his art not merely for emolument, but as a means to copy the Creation. No wonder Goethe, in a rare moment of humility, said of Stichprober's grand design that his own *Wahlverwandschaften* was, by contrast, "mere sums."

In the world of belles lettres, Goethe's comment was anomalous: Stichprober has yet to acquire an appreciative audience, even among such natural soul mates as fans of Adrian Leverkuhn or Cici Chong. Among musicians, however, he is better known. Bach's dismissal aside, pianists of the Romantic and early modern eras were captivated by Castorp's dedication. The book was required reading in both the Viennese and the Leipzig conservatories until the "prepared piano" revolution of the 1950s, and virtually all keyboard artists trained in the Swabian corridor between the wars gratefully acknowledged its influence. Thanks to Dieter Diddle's 1957 translation, Stichprober's book has also affected music on this side of the Atlantic. Among the keyboard giants whom the

Baroque novelist may count among his posthumous protégés are Paolo Chochobare, Finster Willingham, and "Mugwump" Pitts.

The standard English version of the novel is still Diddle's *Temperamental Pianist*. For a recent study that explains Stichprober's neglect as a consequence of "European edginess about ratiocination," see Constance Vickers's august monograph "Castorp on a Hot Tin Roof" in her festschrift for John Cage, *Excuse Me, I Can't Hear You When the Bongo's Running*.

On the Perfectness of the Lord's Heaven *(1681)*

Decrease Mather

The Mather family of Massachusetts Bay made many contributions to emerging American culture, but none so distinctive or so influential as the establishment of the country's first blue laws. They were passed in 1681, following an executive order by magistrate Decrease Mather, and astonishingly they are still on the books; that the Bay State has survived almost three hundred years of dry Sundays has been called, with some justice, "the Massachusetts miracle."

Retailing restrictions are called "blue" laws because the originals were printed on blue paper. Blue because Decrease was obsessed with the color—so much so that a prominent psycho-historian has called him "the most famous azuromaniac in Western history."

Sporting an indigo judicial wig and a cornflower pinned at his collar, munching constantly on blueberry muffins (which he is said to have invented), staring ecstatically at the summer sky, Decrease was a familiar figure in the Bay Colony, as much respected for his staunch Puritanism as he was tolerated for his unusual passion. The tolerance and the respect were related, for Decrease's ideé fixe had a religious cast: a literal believer in Genesis, he claimed, "When God let there be Light, there Appeared the first Visible Sign of His Majesty—and as the Almighty had willed it, the Sign was Blue."

The quotation is from Mather's single book, his self-proclaimed "cerulean theodicy" *On the Perfectness of the Lord's Heaven*. Essentially a proof of God's existence based on the "self-evident perfection" of the blue sky, the book also attempted to justify the unpopular new laws on the grounds that "being Blue, they cannot be Bad." Widely read, it educated many nonscholars about the workings of the Divine Mind, and it did so in precisely the same manner, says religious historian Ditmas Jones, "as stained-glass scenes did for the French serf—by making *visible* what had been unseen."

Jones's appreciation of Mather's work may be colored by his scholarly bias—his remarks appear in his defense of icons, *Why Do You Think They're Called Visions?*—but his argument is still compelling. "Mather humanized the inward Spirit," he explains. "He was the first American to use effectively what I would call the Argument by Natural Phenomena. He saw the sky as proof of a Creator, and was not ashamed to say so, straight out."

The image-hating Puritans did not agree, and Decrease narrowly escaped a heresy trial for what his co-religionists saw as crypto-pantheism. Luckily for him, the Salem troubles of 1691 deflected attention from his theological failings, as the patriarchs swung their hooks toward bigger fish. ("Old Blue" himself condemned the trials because several "witches" had obviously blue eyes.)

Most students of azuromania, unfortunately, have been card-carrying Enzymatics, convinced that all "visionary" insights are the product of chemical imbalances. For a refreshingly anti-Enzymatic approach in which Decrease Mather is mentioned in seven footnotes, see Bessie Nova's virulent monograph on Van Gogh, *Ergotism My Ass: a New Model of Color Obsession*.

One poignant footnote to the Mather story. Decrease died in 1709, on a "birding" trip into Canada. His eyesight failing by that point, he dived to his death into a field of wildflowers, evidently thinking it was the ocean. He is buried in the "Lesser Lights" section of Harvard Cemetery, under a stone with this couplet:

> *May he lie in God's earth where the cornflower grows;*
> *May the bluebird of happiness fly up his nose.*

The White Belt (ca. 1690)

Uku Sensei

This minor classic from Japan's Tokugawa period is the autobiography of the Okinawan martial-arts master Ukoan, known affectionately to his students as Uku Sensei, or Master Uku. Karate specialists have always found it fascinating, not only because of its staunchly lighthearted approach to a deadly art, but also because it demonstrates the Okinawan origin of "the empty hand," an origin frequently disputed by the Japanese. To nonspecialists, and to Western readers in general, Uku's tale holds a broader, almost mystical appeal: The noted historian of trances, Cyril Revels, has commented on its lyrically meditative style, "If John of the Cross hadn't been a wimp, this is the way he would have written." (See Appendix E for an excerpt.)

The title reflects the book's central image: the cloth belt that the young Uku ties around himself both as a way of checking his waistline (he is prone to paunchiness) and as a reminder that "the Way of Heaven runs through the needle's eye." This observation is typically interpreted to mean that progress, whether physical or spiritual, is a process of overcoming restraints—and that the wise man therefore welcomes his privations. But that is only one meaning. Uku wears this "happy shackle" for forty years, and as he ages, the belt ages, too, in a way that augments its symbolic value. Originally white, it gradually becomes so dirty that it is black— and then, as the cloth begins to fade and fray, it becomes gray and then white again. Thus regaining its "infant color," it reflects the journey that the master himself has taken, from "innocent" to "hardened warrior" to "innocent" again. Nietzsche was only one of many nineteenth-century readers who saw in this narrative a figure of the Eternal Return.

Uku wrote the text in the last year of his life, when he knew that his time was at hand. He dedicates the book to his students so that, as he tells them in the preface, "I might leave you with more than *katas* and hardened hands." As intelligently moving as it is, however, the book probably would not have been widely read had Uku not already been famous. In his "hardened warrior" period, as a bodyguard for a Kyoto shogun, he had once disarmed seven pike-wielding assassins, earning himself a reputation as "Invincible Uku" and "the Kyoto Whirlwind." In the late 1600s his Kyoto dojo was the most widely attended in all of Japan, and even aristocrats who despised his Okinawan birth were obliged to acknowledge him as "Sensei of Senseis."

This stoical, visionary teacher was said to have memorized nearly one thousand *katas*, and to have expected of his students that before they donned their own coveted black belts, they be able to demonstrate at least a hundred. His training sessions were so rigorous that in his own cagey estimation, "My students no longer fear death, for they believe they have already died." That attitude of whimsical gravity is Uku's most valuable legacy; it is regrettable that the world knows him only as the father of the karate "belt rank" system.

The Life of Folly (1701)

Anonymous

The anonymity of this caustic allegory was a product not of modesty but of self-protection. In a series of twenty "homiletic sketches," the author gives what he calls a "worm's eye" view of seventeenth-century Massachusetts public figures; his mockery of their vanities and inconsistencies was so severe that, had he revealed himself, he almost certainly would have been "warned out" of the colony. The veiled ridicule of the Mather family is so sweeping that many have supposed Mather-hating Richard Blessing to be the author, but there is no concrete evidence to support the guess.

In each sketch, the main character is given a name that reduces to absurdity one or more of his proclivities. The erudite, scientific-minded Cotton Mather appears as the garrulous, opinionated Little Knowledge; carrying a microscope in one hand and a copy of the real Mather's *Wonders of the Invisible World* in the other, he walks through Boston declaiming at every opportunity, answering with a "perfectly styled sermon" questions such as "Which way to the dunking stool?" Cotton's father, Increase, president of Harvard College, appears as Big Knowledge; he drags a sack of "learned tomes" behind him like the ball and chain of a "wretch condemned to Wisdom," and his conversation is even more ponderous than his son's. Increase's black-sheep brother Decrease is depicted as the glassy-eyed, pontificating Dr. Daydream, whose mania for the color blue compels him to give his children names like Azura and Cobaltus, and to wash his face, three times a day, with blueberry juice.*

The Mathers are not the only celebrities mocked. One of the

* For more on "Blue" Mather, see Mandy Farber, *Color Obsession in Human History*; my sketch in *The Cat's Pajamas*; and page 73 of this volume.

more strident of the Salem witchcraft judges, the irascible Hesketh Grinde, sits in judgment in the book as Jehovah's Trump: his pronouncements from the bench have the "weight of Stone, and may not be Cracked but bye a stumbling Moses." Another magistrate, Richard Tither, compensated for his short stature by donning immense judicial wigs; the allegory has him as Trust-in-Tresses, a "grand Councillor" so tiny that he uses his wig as a feather bed. Samuel Bliss, the renegade minister who had denounced book learning as a Satanic trap, appears as slack-jawed Ignorance (hence our expression "Ignorance is Bliss"). And Roger Williams, who had been warned out to Rhode Island for his "inner light" theories, appears as the Quaboag chieftain Speak-in-Tongues; his enthusiasms on the majesties of the "forest Primeval" are shared by his kinswoman Babbling Brook, modeled on Williams's consort, the Mohawk slave girl Punkaracca.

Condemned by the powerful Mather clan, *The Life of Folly* was almost lost to literary history when forty-nine of the original fifty copies were burned publicly in 1702—as a "gesture of Homage," it was said, to the recently deceased patriarch Increase. The one survivor was spirited away to Providence, where it remained in the Brown University archives until 1811. In that year, as part of a ceremony of rapprochement between the Massachusetts and Rhode Island strains of Puritanism, Brown sent it back to Harvard College. Interestingly, there were still those at the Cambridge institution who felt the rift ought not to be healed: Mather scholar Elizabeth Stricture spoke for this offended minority: "The wicked are not made Godly because they age."

Mother Goose and Father Swine *(1714)*

Victoria Flamande

This crude and yet weirdly amusing "digression" from the tales of
Charles Perrault grew out of the long-standing enmity between
France's *ancien régime* and the rest of Europe. The Low Countries,
like their neighbors to the south and east, had felt the brunt of
Louis XIV's expansionism throughout the seventeenth century, and
literary folk in Bruges were particularly miffed at the cultural dom-
inance of the Sun King's Paris and Versailles. When Perrault published his famous *Tales of Mother Goose* in 1697, appropriating
many motifs from Flemish folklore, he set the stage for an explosion of resentment.

The explosion came in the last year of Louis's reign, and three
years after the Flemish edition of the tales. Flamande was a minor
versifier and town accountant who saw the tales as an opportunity
for a beau geste. Promising to "send back to the frogs better than
they gave," she took the titular heroine of Perrault's book, Mother
Goose, invented a scurrilous companion for her, Father Swine, and

had them trudge the byways of northern Europe in search of their "lost brood"—the fictional characters who had been spirited away by "Louis's lackey."

Among the characters that Flamande called Flemish were Little Red Riding Hood, Sleeping Beauty, and Cinderella. Goose and Swine's search for this trio of "snooty, gallicized ingrates" brings them through a succession of seedy inns and waterfront bars, and this venue affords Flamande the opportunity to employ an almost Regency-style sexual humor. It is doubtful whether this shocked the supposedly prim French as it was meant to, but it did expand Europe's notions of amorous possibility: both "Dutch kissing" and the notorious "Bruges bounce" first saw the light in Flamande's pages. And of course, to many readers the central image of the book—a porcine reprobate squiring around a straitlaced good-wife—was in itself a titillating idea.

After 150 pages of such "experimentation," Goose and Swine locate their lost charges in a Jesuit boarding school south of Paris. Denouncing them for "Romish backsliding" and "secretive congress," they pull them out of the priests' clutches, whip them all

soundly, and send them to bed—but not before delivering a panegyric against priestly machination that is still read, in Belgian schools, as a patriotic classic.

In French translation, Flamande's Francophobic fable reached Paris about 1720, where it was immediately pounced upon as "further evidence" that civilization stopped just west of Lille. Critics denounced the obvious disunities of time and place, and even the mock Rabelaisian aspects of the work failed to generate the pique that Flamande had intended: claiming to be bored rather than shocked, Paris socialites read the book behind closed doors and invented a new phrase for impotence: *l'amour flamandais*.

Gulliver's Travels *(1726)*

Jonathan Swift and Bridget Colley

It is well known that Jonathan Swift, to test the accessibility of his writings to a popular audience, had his Irish housekeeper read them in manuscript, "remorselessly striking from the page" anything she did not immediately understand. The recent discovery of the Trinity College "B Text" to *Gulliver's Travels* indicates that the Dean's humility in this enterprise was even greater than had been supposed, for he permitted his "dear Bridget" to mark the manuscript, making changes whose acute severity bears comparison to the work of Maxwell Perkins and Ezra Pound.

Swift had educated the woman himself, so he may have taken a kind of warped, Frankensteinian pride in her editorial savagery; or he may simply have understood better than his contemporaries the value of what he called a "lean and mean" prose style. Whatever his motivations, following her advice was a bitter pill well taken, for it can hardly be disputed that *Gulliver* is a tighter work for her contempt.

As the sample in Appendix F indicates, the bulk of Colley's changes were minor ones—the cleaning-up of extraneous, elliptical, or flowery language. These in themselves improved the flow of the narrative, but she also made more substantive alterations. Swift admits in a 1727 letter to Stella that "my harpy and sometime saviour Mistress B" had suggested rearranging the order of Lemuel's voyages to provide a "more agreeable introduction to the Fancy." Swift had originally put his caustic Voyage IV first, and Bridget sagely convinced him that "the little people" would provide a snappier opening. She was also influential, as the Trinity manuscript proves, in getting him to change the noble Houyhnhnms from unicorns to the simpler horses.

Colley was not, however, infallible. She could be as peevish as her master, and sometimes obtuse. Her violent scrawls through the Laputa section—virtually obscuring Swift's hand—indicate that, good Catholic that she was, she had scant tolerance for sexual innuendo; while her impassioned entreaty, at the end of the manuscript, that Swift at once "consign to the Hearth yr. cannibalistic and quite *Immodest* Proposal," shows that she completely missed the satire of his pro-Irish tract.

On balance, Colley's revisions made *Gulliver* a more lucid and agreeable book than it might have been. While it is outlandish to suppose, as certain Celtic windbags are now doing, that she was the classic's "real" author, her contribution was considerable, and her defenders may be forgiven for accepting Swift's own characterization of her as "the Galatea who polishes her maker, my better hand."

On the Measurement of Virtue (1731)

Clyde Banks

This brief, animated commentary on Francis Hutcheson's *Inquiry into Beauty and Virtue* (1725) is a monument to the Enlightenment's faith in calculation. Building on Descartes's dream of a "universal mathematical science," Hutcheson had banned the remnants of sentimentalism from Scottish ethics and produced a paragon of that ethometrics which the Germans were calling *das moralische Gesamtkunstwerk* and which Bentham would soon dub the "moral calculus." His student Banks went one step further, assigning numerical values to Hutcheson's tentative formulas, and thus creating, in the estimation of logician Regan Posthaste, "a system for determining right and wrong that, because of its attention to both Categories and Conditions, is at least 7.63 times more reliable than the Ten Commandments."

To compute the morality of an action, Hutcheson had said, one must only gauge the "Degree of Importance of the Action" (I) and then examine it against two propositions. First, that the quantity of "publick Good" (G1) in a given action is the product of the actor's Benevolence (B) and his Abilities (A). Second, that the quantity of "privatte Good" (G2) is the product of Self-Love (S) and Abilities. Taking all these elements into account, and dividing by a necessary Variation factor (V), Hutcheson delivers his final calculation of "Moral Worth" (M), which may be expressed as:

$$M = I/V \times G1 \times G2.$$

Banks's refinement to this scheme was in developing first a quantitative equivalent to each of Hutcheson's basic variables and then a sophisticated catalog of possible human actions, each with its own numerical weighting. Belching in public, for example, was weighted as -1.4; sending a conventional thank-you note was given a 2.0; and self-immolation was a top-of-scale 10. Together, the Banks Catalog (BC) and the Revised Hutcheson Equation (RHE) comprised, in effect, an all-purpose guide to virtuous behavior.

The principal value of the Banks emendation was (and is) its simplicity. It is not exaggerating to say that, with the BC/RHE manual in hand, human beings need no longer exert themselves in that futile speculation over morality that has embroiled and confused the species for thousands of years. In the wise words of

Corrie Bantes, head of the Church of Rational Decision Making (CORD), since 1731 ethical choice has been "as clear-cut as a Euclidean triangle."

Sadly, this assessment is not unanimous. In spite of Banks's stunning achievement, small minds ever since have shunned his message. In 1733, Morris Bodwin denounced him for his "heartless" (but irrefutable!) proof that the life of an author is morally more valuable than that of a chambermaid or a mother—and the nitpicking has gone on ever since. To this baleful state of affairs, Banks's own rejoinder to Bodwin may still be the most appropriate comment: "I assure you, sir, you would change your mind instantly if you could but add and subtract."

Man the Machine (1739)

Jean-Luc Manomètre

The French physician and philosopher Julien La Mettrie has often been called, to use Rose Benét's cliché, "the most notorious materialist of his day." The title really should go to his fellow countryman Manomètre, whose title *L'Homme machine* was borrowed by La Mettrie for his own famous tract, and against whose mechanistic view of human nature the physician's looks quite ephemeral. La Mettrie, in seeking to demonstrate the primacy of matter over "spirit," compared homo sapiens to a complicated piece of machinery. Manomètre had said that the human species literally *was* a machine. The translation of his theory into mere metaphor was, in his shocked summation, "the age's crowning insult to infant Science, from a lackey in the secret service of *l'infame*."

To Manomètre, the human body was not just any machine; it was an "internal combustion" machine whose external correlate was Thomas Newcomen's recently invented steam engine. Like the Newcomen-driven pumps that were beginning to industrialize Europe, the human body "ran" when boiling water turned to steam, the steam drove a cylindrical piston, and the piston drove a rocking or "reciprocating" crossbar attached to the device's other moving parts. Manomètre claimed that the "ticking" sound that doctors traditionally identified as the heart was the sound of this rocking bar—and that the mist that humans breathe out on chilly days was a "residuum" of internal vaporization.

To those who asked why no human dissection had ever revealed anything remotely resembling an inner-body steam engine, Manomètre had an ingenious reply. The engine parts, he explained, were so finely tooled and so meticulously designed for their internal operation that exposure to the air "corrupted" them instantly—just as the machine's "lubricating oil," its obviously blue blood, turned to red upon meeting "the coarse element."

As Manomètre's language implies, there was more to his theory than simple materialism. In his insistence on the "exquisite specialization" of the human machine—its "sublime fitness for its place, and no other," he was evoking the subtly nonmaterialistic image of the Divine Craftsman, or "watchmaker God," which materialists like La Mettrie denied. The underlying message of his book was a religious one: that the apparent corruptibility of human life was a mirage, and that in our deepest selves (what he liked to call our "pump of pumps"), we are the "perfectly oiled contraptions of an engineer who does not make mistakes (*l'ingénieur infaillible*").

At death, Manomètre suggested, God gathered the "shattered cogs of this dim realm" together into an endlessly efficient celestial factory. But he never quite figured out why the machine should run down in the first place, and he was at work on a sequel—in part a response to La Mettrie, in part an analysis of "inefficient vaporization," or poor nutrition—when he died in 1750. La Mettrie followed him one year later, uttering on his deathbed the plaintive cry, "I sure hope that loony was right."

The Heth Material (1740–42)

Joice Heth

This American slave's journal illustrates how in literary history one fallacy often overtakes another. Only the very innocent today accept the hoary tale of George Washington and the cherry tree as anything but a pretty fabrication. Many, however, accept unquestioningly that the fabricator was one Mason Locke Weems, the nutty parson who wrote Washington's biography in 1799. It's true that Weems popularized the anecdote, but as the Heth Material makes quite clear, neither Washington nor Weems was the originator of the deathless line "I cannot tell a lie."

Heth, a Ghanaian woman who served as George's nurse for two years, kept a diary of her tenure in an idiosyncratic, charming patois. First published in 1961, it concerns mostly domestic trivialities, such as her charge's resistance to Saturday-night baths, his insouciant glibness, and his intermittent torture of insects. But there is also much of interest to the developmental psychologist, such as a description of the Washington household as "one kinnde of hollyplace [she means "shrine"] to the great chief over water, they calle him Geo." This picture of our first president's devoutly (and according to Heth, somewhat oppressively) Tory childhood may help to explain his willingness, later in life, to lead rebels against "our father the King."

Most importantly, there is the tree story, which bears quoting in full. This is the entry for March 19, 1741, when the young Virginian was just nine years old:

> *Small master he today bee verry Wikked. He chop chop Big Master's berry tree, saye to Mistress Marcy what he do, what he do nowe he assk her verry shaking, be affeard of Big Master. M. Marcy tellem, No makem storry like you do, your fadder see thru him. Tellem truth, say I cannot lye to you oh my loved*

fadder, that bee best waye saving your skin. So Small Master do like shee tellem and lucky too. Big Master crye and bee happie, little Master hee bee so brave. Next I cut taters wronge way I assk M. Marcy shee make mee up onne like good storry.

The Heth style here is, of course, marvelous in its own right, but the passage is also interesting for public reasons. First, it shows a Washington that no biographer has ever painted—calculating and self-serving. Second, it shows that the "Weems version" was not original, but lifted directly from Joice Heth—or to be more precise, from Heth's account of George's conspiratorial chat with "Mistress Marcy." Nobody knows who this playmate might have been, but it was clearly she who gave the culprit his exculpatory zinger.

Circumstantial evidence clinches the point. In 1835, when Heth was touring with P. T. Barnum's road show, she gave the showman a curriculum vitae for promotional purposes. That document is now on exhibit at Chicago's Circus Hall of Fame. Not surprisingly, it has her at the Washington family's Wakefield estate in 1741 and 1742; but it also has her, in the summer of 1795, as the cleaning lady for one "Mason Locke," an itinerant preacher from Beaufort, South Carolina. Whether the enterprising Weems picked her trunk lock or merely her brain is inconsequential: clearly, he did not invent his best tale.

The Sneezing Potion *(1746)*

Aristide Forestière

Forestière's satirical drama *La Potion Eternuante* provides a rare instance in literary history of a sequel more successful than the original. In 1747, as Parisian theater society was just beginning to tire of the sentimental, moralizing *comédies larmoyantes* that had dominated the stage for a decade, Forestière produced his first "weeping play," and was roundly denounced for ineptitude: the ever-sobbing characters of his *Pleure-moi un fleuve* ("Cry Me a River") were too lacrimal even for Paris. To revenge himself on an unappreciative public, he followed this flop with a sardonic, farcical "sneezing drama"—which, much to his surprise, made him rich.

Where the characters of the typical *comédie larmoyante* weep dramatically over domestic conundrums, the hero of Forestière's farce, Jacques Benisse, is an incessant sneezer. To ingratiate himself with a smart set, he begins taking snuff, until he develops an allergy that has him ah-chooing every time he speaks. The plot unfolds around his attempts to find a cure for his initially humorous but soon objectionable condition, and in particular to locate a special potion that he is told the "Red Indians" use.

Forestière makes much of the similarity between *potion* (potion) and *potin* (gossip). Because he must speak to ask for help, and because speaking triggers the affliction, Jacques's conversations are a series of interruptions, and his questions about the potion are often interpreted as requests for the day's juicy gossip. This conceit allows Forestière the opportunity to have his characters spread tales about each other and about real Parisians of the time. During the play's three-year run, the author revised it periodically to include rumors about Madame Poisson's latest lover or the Duc d'Ennui's impending bankruptcy. Its popularity clearly was due in part to the audience's expectation of fresh scandals.

Much of the topical banter is obscure now, although the play retains its lively, coarse humor, and Jacques himself remains an endearing buffoon. According to Forestière expert Terence Deladier, *The Sneezing Potion* is "still a sure thing for amateur productions, if you can find an actor with the physical stamina to pull it off." This comment has been echoed by countless directors who have begun rehearsals only to discover, weeks into production, that repeated sneezing has caused their star to adopt the listless twitching known to the medical world as the Benisse Syndrome. Indeed, to professional actors, the part of Jacques has always been a *sommet du métier*, like Odile's thirty-two *fouettés* in *Swan Lake*. In this century, says Deladier, the only performer to be truly made for the part was "the ingenious beast" Antonin Artaud.

The Toddler *(1757–61)*

James Pregfoot and Roger Barenant

Pregfoot and Barenant were schoolmasters in Bath who gained a celebrity far beyond that provincial capital with this series of "Moral Readings for the Young," issued quarterly over a four-year span. Alarmed by the popularity of Richardson's *Clarissa Harlowe* and its many imitations, the two inaugurated their project with a broadside against such "vellum-bound syrups" and the announced intention to "present to our nation's most prized treasure, viz. its youth, so ample and characteristic a record of the stream of the world's thought that each reader's mind shall be enriched, refined, and fertilised by it." Beginning in April of 1757, they fulfilled that intention each season by publishing a new, sixty-four page collection of famous poems, essays, and dramatic sketches.

Most of the *Toddler* pieces were gleaned from the works of established authors, from the Greek dramatists to Alexander Pope. Occasionally, however, the two masters included efforts of their own, which revealed them as mordant if mundane versifiers. In *Toddler 5*, for example, Barenant offered his young readers this example of "false tho diverting rhyme":

> You shake and shake the pickle bottle.
> Nothing comes, and then a lot'll.

While in *Toddler 12*, Pregfoot, who always had a penchant for riddles, gave this oblique definition of an egg:

> A chest without lock or key or lid;
> Yet golden treasure inside is hid.

That P&B (as their adoring public knew them) considered such trifles of greater literary value than the "maundering simplicities" of the sentimental novelists suggests, perhaps, the relative worth they placed on "right thinking" and felicity of expression. Philosophically the *Toddler*'s authors were vehemently conventional, taking it as an article of faith that Western civilization was the diadem of planetary achievement and Great Britain its central jewel. Their popular "Narrow Path" column counseled sobriety, stoicism, and love of tradition; and their principal objection to the Richardson school was that it portrayed vice and virtue side by side, "without sufficient Discrimination being employed such that the Untutored might not go Astray."

Aside from helping to entrench kneejerk anglophilia, the *Toddler* also had profound social effects, particularly in the fashion arena. Pregfoot and Barenant were among the first English publishers to use line engravings as didactic illustration, and they were doubly inventive at the time because they represented "morally instructive" characters as children dressed in contemporary adult styles. Part of the odd charm of the work today is in seeing Horatio at the bridge as a ten-year-old in knee breeches and a periwig, or the faithful Old Testament wife Ruth as a pubescent girl with décolletage and a mole. The contemporary painterly conceit of depicting children as miniaturized adults may be traced directly to the P&B vogue.

Whig-hating critics have always been hard on "the boys from Bath." Geoff Klink, writing in the *Marx-Lenin Fashion Quarterly*, called them "point men for retrograde fopocracy," and even their admirers have had to admit that the duo had intolerant tendencies (see particularly their tirades against the gavotte in *Toddler 14* and *15*). But it is hard to condemn entirely a production that first published Goldsmith's "Goody Two-Shoes," or that was responsible for the famous characterization of Dr. Johnson as "the Great Khan of English literature."

The Letter Q *(1759)*

"Jacques"

The year 1759 was a notable one in French letters. April saw the appearance of Voltaire's *Candide*, June the Jesuit-inspired suppression of Diderot's *Encyclopédie*, and November a *scandale littéraire* surrounding a lexicographical bagatelle called *The Letter Q*. Ostensibly an unauthorized "addendum" to Diderot's work, it extended the rebellious tendencies of the *philosophes* to blatant lengths by providing satirical definitions of "all Académie-approved vocabulary between *pythonisse* and *rabâchage*."

Pythonisse and *rabachage* were respectively the last *P* word and the first *R* word in the Académie's official dictionary, but they were also politically loaded code terms. Louis XIV's mistress Madame de Maintenon had been called "the Pythoness" in her day, and *rabâchage* was Parisian slang for "courtly twaddle." So the anti-noble bias was clear from the beginning.

The entries did not soften its edge. *Quai* was not "quay" or "wharf" but the "honest man's buffet, where he dines without tipping the waiter"—a reference to dockside fishing, which provided sustenance for Paris's poor. *Question* was not "question" but the rack—the torture device used in the Bastille and other prisons to "put the question" (*mettre la question*) to enemies of the Crown. *Quotité*, or "quota," was a specific quota: "the 110 percent of the honest man's earning which is legally owed to the crown."

This attack on privilege did not delight the king. Within twenty-four hours of its appearance, *La Lettre Q* was condemned as treasonous, and reading it made a capital crime. It circulated widely *sub rosa*, however, and had a disturbing effect; many of the *philosophes* expressed chagrin that the writer had violated the satirist's first law of self-preservation by so baldly removing the velvet glove. Diderot complained to a friend that "this odious screed will get us all killed."

The editor of the *Encyclopédie* had good cause to be anxious, for many suspected he was the anonymous Jacques; the king was known to have compiled an "enemies list" of other possible culprits, including Voltaire. Thanks to computer analysis conducted by Dr. Darius Dadadisque of the Palo Alto Center for Lexical Disarray, we now know that the author-publisher was one Charles d'Evremont, a count who had lost a coveted sinecure and issued the work in revenge. Recombinant delta lexication showed that only d'Evremont or a nineteenth-century baker named George Swillings-Pond could possibly have created the manuscripts, and since Swillings-Pond had not yet been born, the authorship became obvious.

Dadadisque's ingenuity has even provided us with biographical details. "Internal evidence makes it clear," he writes in his introduction to the text, "that the author was a bitter and obsessed individual whose life had been ruined by the letter *Q*. In the year 1757, he had bought the exclusive rights to distribute *quenelles*—those delicate fish balls so prized by the aristocracy—at court functions in Paris and at Versailles. Somehow the royal license was awarded to a rival, and d'Evremont was left, as his coded introduction makes clear, with four thousand pounds of rotten cod. Hence his definition of *quenelle* as 'a poisonous mush.' "

Historian Bebe Rossiter gives Jacques high marks in her critique of the *philosophes* as closet reactionaries, *Face-Lifting the Ancien Régime*. Dadadisque's detective work is described in *Weighing the Evidence: Word Density and its Relation to Authorship*. That volume also explains the recombinant system in detail, gives the specific gravity of over two thousand Indo-European roots, and contains a free floppy disk.

The Weather War (1764)

Gertrude Bastling

The author of this early science-fiction novel was, in her own estimation, "a baroness by birth, indolent by inclination, and a writer by *force majeur*." Reputedly a mistress of Frederick II and verifiably the confidante of Voltaire, she spent the first forty years of her life as a "pampered court appendage" (her words again) and then, having learned from her doctors that she would die within a year from pneumoconiosis, turned with fierce dedication to her writing table so that "my legacy might be more distinguished than the memory of a thousand minuets." Her single-mindedness created *Der Wetterkrieg*, whose success she did not live to enjoy.

Brisk in plot but somber in mood, *The Weather War* tells the tale of two central European duchies, Kvetchtal and Braunschweig, who are rivals for the tourist trade of Paris and London. They are situated in a lowland plain with frequently shifting cloud forma-

tions, and since the travelers whose business they are wooing pre-
fer sunshine to shadow, prosperity falls each season to that duchy
which has been blessed with better weather. As the novel opens,
the Landgraf of Braunschweig, dissatisfied with the chanciness of
this situation, decides to weight the scales in his favor with the
help of a gigantic wind machine. As the tourist season approaches,
he sets the device on his region's highest mountain, points it toward Kvetchtal, and blows all his clouds in their direction.

This action is the first sally in the "weather war." Kvetchtal soon
constructs its own wind machine, retaliates by drenching Braunschweig with rain, and sends flyers throughout Europe announc-
ing itself as "the undisputed Sun-master of the universe."
Braunschweig picks up the gauntlet, builds a bigger wind machine,
enlists the entire population in its operation, and sends back the
clouds—which elicits an equal reaction from Kvetchtal, and so on,
until in Bastling's sly description, "every man, woman, and child
in both duchies is spending twenty-five hours a day blowing wind."
Naturally, this wreaks havoc on both economies, social peace is
utterly destroyed, and the horde of tourists that the rivals had
hoped to attract makes its way instead to tiny Abendland, "which
is too poor to afford the blessings of modern machinery, and must
make do with the sun that God provides."

Bastling's satire was directed not only at the inanity of politi-
cians, but also at the blind belief in progress and in its hand-
maiden, "our own golden calf," science. Like Voltaire, she was
suspicious of the "sunshine philosopher" Gottfried Leibnitz, but
where Voltaire had questioned his concept of perfection, Bastling
went further, ridiculing the idea of improvement itself. Her outlandish devices are designed "to better the lot that God has given";
they function thus as blasphemous mockeries of the eighteenth
century's faith in machinery. No doubt the negative view of science displayed here reflected a bitterness at her own physicians'
impotence.

Frogs Go Home (1767)

"Stephen Razin"

Under Catherine the Great's reign of "enlightened despotism" (1762–96), Russia endured a process of westernization—or more precisely gallification—which made French the unofficial state language and led one contemporary to quip that "by court decree the headwaters of the Volga have now been extended to Paris." The empress herself was personally responsible for much of this. A friend of Voltaire and Diderot, she purchased the latter's vast library, sent money to several of the *philosophes*, and in 1767, under the spell of their liberal ideas, even convened a legislative commission designed to soften the asperities of Russian law.

In this latter step, according to some Russians, she had gone too far. In the fall of that year, in response to the quite meager advances of the commission (torture, for example, was "restricted"), Muscovites were intrigued by an anonymous pamphlet denouncing the imperial reforms and blaming "frog eaters from Hell" for reducing Mother Russia to "Liberty's charwoman." Diderot was singled out as a "secret nephew of Ramona" (Ramona Vislyevich was a notorious Moscow pickpocket) and, in an ironic taunt at the empress's sexual appetite, as "the seducer of virgins." If Russia wished to regain her former eminence as the "third Rome," the pamphleteer admonished, she must "send the powdered croakers packing," strike the "L word" from her vocabulary, and hew to traditional Russian values.

There was nothing particularly new about this line. A minority cabal in Catherine's circle had long distrusted foreign influence, and even the orthographic quip was merely a variant on a theme: to traditionalists, the letter that now represented *libéralisme* had earlier stood for Alexei Lobachev, the reviled opponent of the partition of Poland. What was unusual was the use of "Stephen Razin" as a cover for the author's "Russia first" views.

Razin had led a serf rebellion between 1667 and 1671, and following his execution had become a folk hero, the image of latent peasant power. The use of this famous figure as the mouthpiece for antiliberalism—for, in effect, *more* repression—struck many readers as an "aristocratic trick," designed to sully Razin's reputation. Others, taking the right-wing message as ironic, saw the martyred Razin as an ideal spokesman for neo-isolationism: in Mikhail Bugakov's recent assessment of the *Frogs* incident, the pamphlet served as a Russian "Modest Proposal," "which only the congenitally retrograde could interpret as heartfelt."

There is reason to believe that both partisan readings miss the point, and that *Frogs Go Home* was an outburst of xenophobia pure and simple. Louise Masterson develops this point intelligently in her study of modern nationalism, *The New Altar*, where she links the Razin affair to the anti-Byronist sentiments of nineteenth-century Italy and Greece. "Phrases from the Razin manuscript (distributed maliciously through Europe by Diderot) are echoed in the Mediterranean *Limey Go Home* screeds, and there are entire passages repeated in the Italian attack on Byron, *Piccolo Giorgio, o il conte falso*." One may observe the same distrust of foreign influence, of course, in England (the *Good-bye, Wogs* writings of the Hanoverian age) and in North America (the *Everybody Go Home* works of the 1850s).

The Public Burning *(1770s?)*

Voltaire (?)

The manuscript of this tragicomic attack on religious intolerance was discovered in Voltaire's papers at his death, and it was originally thought to be from his pen. Nineteenth-century graphologists disputed the handwriting, however, and since then numerous scholars—pointing to the occasionally pedestrian style as well as the uncharacteristically dotted *i*'s (they appear as ♡)—have attributed the piece to Eustache Berne, the master's literate gardener at Ferney.

Whoever wrote it, *L'Auto-da-fé publique* certainly displays Voltairean qualities. Presented as a *"fable amorale et historique,"* it concerns the "purification by fire" of two fourteenth-century heretics, the English reformer John Wycliffe and his Czech follower John Hus. Both men, condemned by the Council of Constance (1415–18), were condemned to the stake. Executing Hus was not problematic, for he obligingly attended the council himself to defend his antipapal position. Burning Wycliffe was more difficult, as he had died in 1384, under a cloud of censure, but still officially, if ironically, in the Roman fold. The dark humor of the Ferney manuscript grows from the exhumation, excommunication, and ultimate conflagration of what amounts to a shroud of his bones.

The principal carriers of that humor are the two gravediggers entrusted with delivering Wycliffe's remains to the Constance ecclesiastical court. They are called Omelette and Haricot—obvious corruptions of Hamlet and Horatio—and the parodic element of their speech is evident from their initial appearance, when Omelette admits, "Alas poor Yorker, I knew him not, Haricot." In their banter they treat the bones as if they were alive, expressing both scorn for their sins and pity for their impending fate. When Wycliffe's remains are at last consigned to the flames, and reduced to ashes within minutes, Haricot's dryly malicious response is, "That's the quickest dust to dust I've ever seen."

But such graveside quips are only part of the volume's appeal. On a pictorial level, the narrative has been likened to Brueghel's hell paintings and Goya's *Horrors of War*. In the Hus burning scene especially, the language is that of sharp and sensual contrasts:

> *The spectators, some tar-streaked in mock mourning, some florid*
> *with wine, others bearing daffodils like scepters of innocence,*

swelled toward the stake now under the gray April heaven, their murmurings of marvel mixing with the shrieks of the unfortunate Bohemian in an antiphony that the hills of Italy had missed since the scorching of Savonarola. Rain dusted the faggots as they burst into flower, and the hissing of the wood joined the chorus, so that in all of inconstant Constance, no sound was more pleasing to monkish ears than this Dies Irae hummed like Carnival.

On a theological level as well, the work is compelling. Both Wycliffe and Hus had been condemned partly because of their rejection of transubstantiation—the doctrine that contends Christ is present in the Eucharist not just symbolically but in fact. The Ferney manuscript, which incidentally characterizes Christian communion as "a bizarre vestige of cannibalism," likens this once-critical question to "the other pressing issue of the time: whether God speaks himself in the thunder, or uses a trumpet." On the question of papal indulgences, Voltaire comments that at any price they are a cheat, or more precisely, "a priest in a poke." And with regard to the council's posthumous excommunication of Wycliffe, he observes that this indicates *chronoclasme*, or "time-breaking."* "Is it not blasphemous," asks the "wise dunce" Haricot, "to send to Hell on this gray afternoon a soul that God has judged so long ago?"

The play on time was of course a subtle reference to the deist "conviction" that God, if he existed, was an *orologue*. And the use of the metaphor suggested, perhaps, a pietistic side to Voltaire—a side that could actually take offense at the notion of the Watchmaker being mocked. It was exactly this hint of religiosity that led scholars to favor Berne (a soi-disant Huguenot) over his avowedly atheist master.

The Invisible Thumb *(1780)*

Henry Cheshire

Adam Smith's doctrine of the beneficent "invisible hand" that turns competitive self-interest into public gain is a cornerstone of free-market economics, so familiar to the semiliterate through repetition that one can summon up the entire laissez-faire edifice with a passing utterance of this code phrase. This was true in the eighteenth century as well. In spite of the enormous effect that *The Wealth of Nations* had on European politics and economics, most readers were able to reduce the Scotsman's arguments to a fundamental gratifying message: "Publick good" is the result of private strife, regulated mysteriously into beneficence by Smith's "hand."

Cheshire, a professor of "moral economy" at Edinburgh, took advantage of this oversimplification of his countryman's magnum

* "Chronoclasm" was a cult religion in the years between Voltaire's death in 1778 and the French Revolution. Its rituals involved the turning-back of clock hands, to suggest that a new order of "timeless bliss" was on the horizon. That the democratic revolutionaries he spawned should have adopted the name of his "Romish cabal" would have astounded the sage of Ferney.

opus to draft a good-natured critique called *The Invisible Thumb*. Where Smith had stressed the advantages of an unregulated economy, Cheshire pointed to its abuses: dramatic income differentials, the rapid "enclosure" of the countryside, absence of job security, and a prevailing attitude toward "the lower orders" that permitted fourteen-hour workdays for children of twelve. Sure, there was an invisible hand at work, he admitted; but it worked to disrupt, not harmonize, public relations.

Putting Smith's own metaphor to good effect, Cheshire wrote that the trouble lay not with "the Hand itself, but with its damaged, and one must confess, Opposing, thumb." In Cheshire's conceit, the hand, although invisible, was identifiable: it belonged to the deists' "absentee Landlord," who had been using it "since the days of Saint Fugger" to regulate European industry and commerce. The problem was that in "hammering out the Infrastructure of the Industrial Revolution," the well-meaning autocrat had smashed his thumb, and ever since then his celestial management had been "less than Dextrous." Hence sweatshops, bankruptcies, and starving urchins.

Cheshire's bagatelle enjoyed a vogue in the 1780s, and had an effect on, among others, the young David Ricardo. Most Smithites wrinkled their noses at it in mild displeasure, but the master himself was not so sanguine. In 1784 he sued Cheshire for metaphor infringement. The ensuing litigation dragged on for years, and was only halted by Smith's death in 1790.

The British proletarian gesture of nose-thumbing, incidentally, dates from the turn of the century, and is a direct evocation of Cheshire. Both it, and the far ruder gesture of jabbing a thumb in another's direction, were originally class-based insults. To "thumb" someone, in the 1820s, was the equivalent of our "giving him the finger."

Demopolis *(1782)*

Etienne d'Embonpoint

D'Embonpoint, the "Popinjay of Poissy," wrote this pro-Royalist, dystopian "travelogue" in reaction to the American Revolution. Cornwallis surrendered at Yorktown in October of 1781; six months later *Demopolis; ou, une voyage aux régions des canailles* explained to d'Embonpoint's freethinking countrymen what would follow from this "tragedy" in twenty years.

A half-Bourbon on his mother's side, d'Embonpoint was morbidly fearful of democracy, and in *Demopolis* (the title means "the people's city"), he spared no venom in exposing its potential ills. In the year of the voyage, 1801, North America had become a disaster zone. Its citizens, the self-proclaimed "new men," were brutish *célébrants du vulgarité* whose entertainments ran from torture to daylong intoxication, and who "can only be described as *canaille*"—a barnyard coin that means, roughly, "pig folk." The novel begins with the execution of a Tory family who have unwisely returned from Canada to New York; it ends in a "swinish *bellum omnium contra omnes*" where the pig folk "rut unconscionably after each other's sows" and spend the entire afternoon on all fours.

Voltaire had quipped of Rousseau's primitivism that he could not wait to get on all fours; the echo of that famous joke here was both a private taunt and a public warning, for d'Embonpoint was convinced that, left to their own "rebel snortings," the Americans would soon revert to savagery: "it is civilization itself they cannot stomach."* In the dozens of feuilletons where he advertised his

---

* Another Bourbonist, Chateaubriand, who was sixteen years' d'Embonpoint's junior, is often credited with having called the United States "the only nation in history to have gone from barbarism to decadence without passing through the intermediate stage of civilization." The original speaker was the narrator of *Demopolis*.

book, he pleaded with the *philosophes* to "embrace true Reason, not its slavering, egalitarian, phantom double," and to denounce the popular belief in human perfectibility. Only respect for traditional hierarchies, he was certain, could save France from following America "down the sewer."

This embittered Hobbesian may have erred in predicting "the fury of Demos" for the United States, but he was fatally right about France. After a season as the literary darling of Marie Antoinette (she kept his book by her bedside at the Petit Trianon), he retired, still fretting, to his Poissy chateau, where he tried to live in a *style quatorzienne*, with dozens of liveried servants and a private zoo. There, in 1791, the Revolution found him, and there Marat himself pronounced a death sentence. D'Embonpoint went to the guillotine in July. His biographer, Marie Chrétien du Plessy-Ferguson, tells us that his withering last words were *"Jean-Jacques, tu vieille salope, aussi ce que j'ai dit!"* ("Jean-Jacques, you old bitch, I told you so!").

Collectors *(1796)*

Wilhelm von Grinzenbrecher

The fame of this collection of stories rests exclusively on the initial tale, "Kopferzahlen" (Head Count), which concerns the underground museum of the nobleman Rickardus Aachenspiel, containing the severed heads of over two hundred executed dignitaries. The story, which appeared first in 1793, at the height of the French Revolution's Terror, was interpreted as an attack on democratic excesses, and this reading is lent weight by the fact that Aachenspiel's trophies include the heads of Jean Marois ("Little Robespierre") and a lady-in-waiting to Marie Antoinette. But the count's calmly reasoned vindication of his passion, presented to his shocked visitor Abram van Helsing, gives a broader philosophical import to the tale: the collector's most subtle observation is that van Helsing, who is appalled at "brutality's evidence," is yet an enthusiast of the revolutionary fervor that has made much of his collection possible.

Other stories in the collection also hint at a bizarre sensibility. In "The Peanut Men," for example, von Grinzenbrecher tells the tale of Ilsa Laszlo, a Slovakian peanut farmer's daughter who uses her collection of "drawn and halved" peanuts—with the internal "Santa" thus exposed—as a training aid in physiognomy. The gentle mockery of that contemporary pop-psychology fad peaks at the end of the story, where Ilsa demonstrates the "transcendental unity of apperception" and the "fundamental monotony of humankind" by mashing her entire collection into peanut butter.

Von Grinzenbrecher was a part-time harpsichordist, and his musical passions are evident in "The Stradivarius" and "The Instrument That No One Could Play." In the former, he traces the influence of Stradivarius Number 109 as it passes from one owner to another, wreaking curious vengeance on all who attempt to plumb its mysteries. In the latter, another obsessive collector, Byron Southey, squanders his friendships and his fortune in bringing back from the Amazon a "stringed drum" that seems to play itself, but that is insensitive to human operation. In "Drawing the Tree," a different kind of obsession is explored. Mario Cacona, a draftsman, is convinced that if he can reproduce the "essence" of a plane tree in his front yard, he will become "as rooted and eternal" as his subject. This post-Kantian, crypto-mystical expectation becomes the "plummeting design" of his life, as he spends hours drawing the tree in different lights.

What links all these tales together is von Grinzenbrecher's evident conviction that obsession is the governing motive of human behavior. Marxist critics, focusing on the "acquisitive urge" that permeates so many of the stories, have seen him as a "secret critic" of the "post-industrial, anal order." Less programmatic readers have seen foreshadowings of Edgar Allen Poe and Stephen King. The Poe connection is not outlandish, although it may be going a bit far to announce, as Matilda Kirschenbaum has done, that "the entire dungeon mise-en-scène of *The Cask of Amontillado* is a deft but obvious borrowing from the 'Kopferzahlen.'"

The Discovery of Ceres (1804)

Giuseppe Piazzi

Piazzi was an Italian monk and astronomer who, in 1801, discovered the first of the so-called minor planets—the bodies we today know as asteroids. He named it after the Roman grain goddess Ceres and, in spite of its tiny size relative to the six known planets, attempted to get it officially recognized as the *pianeta settima*. In this he was frustrated by what he saw as "the machinations of entrenched interests"; *La scoperta di Ceres* is the impassioned, occasionally delusional, but consistently enlightening account of his travails.

Twenty years before Piazzi's discovery, the German-born English astronomer William Herschel had spotted the first new planet since ancient times. We know it today as Uranus, but Herschel's original name for it was Sidus Georgium, or "George's Star"—an eponymous nod to George III. In choosing this modern tag, Herschel implied his liberation from the backwardness of the ancient world, and established what he hoped would be a tradition of naming celestial bodies for Earth's celebrities (he named one Uranian moon "Hersch"). Piazzi was entirely at odds with this type of labeling. Arguing that the heavenly bodies had been spinning far longer than our "mental wheels" (*ruote mentali*), he refused the British Academy's suggestion—made in a snide congratulatory letter—that he call his discovery Charles Emmanuel, after the current ruler of Sardinia, and chauvinistically stuck by his "good Latin name."

But his tiff with the British establishment was only part of Piazzi's problems with protocol. Even at home, adulation was hardly forthcoming, for the monk was a native of backward Sicily and a professor at the island's newly founded University of Palermo. Northern Italian scholars, whose universities were five hundred years old, dismissed "the stargazing Palerman" as an upstart, a possible charlatan, a *cafone d'occhi grandi*, or "big-eyed yokel." The poignancy of his narrative is particularly intense when he laments the rejection of those he counted on as colleagues: "From the Teutons I had not expected civility, and consequently was not disappointed; but the lances forged at home cut me deeply."

Piazzi never got his planetary designation, although the European scientific community did accept the name Ceres, and both the Paris and Greenwich observatories offered him temporary positions. His memoir remains a unique perspective on the infighting of Enlightenment scientists: in the estimation of Peter Gray, "The shoddy treatment that the Sicilian endured makes Galileo's troubles look like chopped liver."

Miseries of Human Life (1806)

James Beresford

The year 1806 saw not only the establishment of the Continental System, by which Napoleon sought to crush British maritime hegemony with an early version of the Common Market, but also the publication of several "misery collections" demonstrating what Paul Dickson calls "the inherent perversity of things." At a time when the increasingly porphyric George III was expected to absent the throne any moment for his gadabout son the Prince of Wales, British subjects took from these books of anticonsolation the kind of pleasure (as Sinclair Lewis said in another context) that "one has in sucking an aching tooth." "If the monarchy was soon to pass from an idiot to a clown," wrote Basil Wilkins of the "miseries" vogue, "wry obeisance to the goddess Discord seemed in order."

Most of these books have been lost to time, and we know of their existence only by reference. Thanks to the assiduous work of Dickson's researchers, however, one such classic has come to light. Published by William Miller, the "Cheapside Caxton," it appeared under the long-winded title *The Miseries of Human Life or the Groans of Samuel Sensitive and Timothy Testy*; Dickson shows, on exquisitely ephemeral evidence, that the dual authorship concealed the identity of James Beresford, an Oxford historian best known for his study *The Wooden Age: New Light on the Ancient-Modern Flap*.

Among the situations to which Beresford turned his singularly jaundiced eye were the following:

- Being requested by a foreigner who understands very little of the English language, to hear him read Milton.
- Writing upon a thin sheet of paper, very small crumbs of bread under it.
- Upon returning from a Tour to the Continent, being asked by everyone you meet for *your private opinion of things in general*.
- Striking your foot against another step after you had concluded that you had reached the top of the stairs.
- Trying to pass a man who waddles.

And so on, through 176 pages, each entry more dyspeptic than the last, each designed to prove Beresford's coy contention that "If the world is a Watch, as the Deists claim, then it is evidently two minutes behind."

To anyone who wants a corrective to galloping optimism, Beresford's book is as good an emetic as can be found. In its modest way it is as distinguished an attack on the Panglossian delusion as

Candide or Bastling's *Weather War*. The scholarly world owes a debt to Mr. Dickson for having focused its attention on this rotten plum, and I for one am delighted to applaud him.

I must confess that I am rather less enthusiastic about his suggestion that Beresford's contemporary, Robert Heron, was responsible for the companion volume *More Miseries*, which appeared over the name Sir Fretful Murmur. Heron died in 1800 of liver failure, and as B. R. Camembert said to me recently over artichokes, "Even Heron, with his indefatigable energy, would have had difficulty pushing a pen six years down."

Lord Gout's Legions *(1809)*

Gottfried Harnsaur

In this brilliantly narrow-minded historical treatise, the Mainz physician and gout sufferer Harnsaur speculated on what the world would be like without his illness. "The pages of history virtually shudder," he wrote, "with the accomplishments of the gout-ridden; had so many giants of the chronicle not been afflicted, we would not now be facing our current pass."

By current pass, Harnsaur meant Napoleonic invasion. His hometown had recently fallen to the emperor's armies, and his book, written in the officially proscribed *plattmainzisch* dialect, was on one level a patriotic flourish: he sought to show that the "Corsican popinjay's" stunning victories were "compensatory feats" (*Entschadigunsgrosstäte*) against the depression brought on by the disease. Thus the entire map of Europe, with its French empire from Warsaw to Trafalgar, had been indirectly drawn by Graf Gicht, or "Lord Gout."

Harnsauer's proto-Freudian interpretation was dead wrong in the case of Napoleon, for there is no evidence that he suffered from gout. This does not, however, discredit the doctor's thesis, for his other examples are well documented. Both Luther and Calvin, for example, had the debilitating malady, and while Harnsauer certainly goes too far in suggesting that "uric acid was the ultimate conquerer of papal privilege," it is difficult to argue with his more modest conclusion that, had the two reformers been healthy, "the dyspeptic element in the Great Reformation might have been softened and, with it, the movement itself."

Similarly, with regard to Isaac Newton, the doctor grinds his ax a little thin, claiming that the entire Scientific Revolution was the product not of the Englishman's large brain, but of his swollen ankles. Newton's early dream of being a cavalry officer, he says, was frustrated only by the disease—so that without the "enriching taxation" (*bereicherende Besteurung*) of Graf Gicht, the course of human thought would have been dramatically slowed down.

Harnsauer's most compelling example rests on the intertwined stories of William Pitt and Benjamin Franklin. Pitt's attempts to ameliorate Parliament's treatment of the American colonies were thwarted on at least two occasions by attacks of the disease; on the first occasion the result was the Boston Tea Party, on the other the Battle of Bunker Hill. Franklin's part in prewar negotiations was also interrupted by painful episodes, so that one must take as only slightly exaggerated Harnsauer's depiction of Lord Gout as a secret Minuteman, or his facetious comment that gout should be proclaimed the American "national disease."

To professional historians of his era, Harnsauer was a mere oddity, but today's "glandular historiographers" see him as a founding father. Keppel's biography and Winterthur's psycho-historical monograph have both served to earn him wider attention, and the 1991 meeting of the Annus Mirabilis League will be devoted to the year 1809. Harnsauer knew, of course, that it marked the publication of his book and the ill-fated War of Austrian Liberation; something he could not know, but which would have pleased him immensely, was that it also marked the birth of Charles Darwin—another of Lord Gout's famous victims.

Hesperides the Aarborg (1820)

Nils Norresund

The inherent charm of this modern Danish folk tale has always been overshadowed by partisan debates over its authorship. The first such debate occurred in the 1820s, when its eighty-year-old author was accused by the Heidelberg Academy of "confiscating at least an emblem, and perhaps an entire work" from their lamented star writer, the poet Novalis. Novalis had died in 1801, leaving behind a rich legacy of Romantic tales and the unfinished novel *Heinrich von Ofterdingen*, which used a blue flower to symbolize spiritual longing. Because Norresund (like many other writers) adopted this symbol for his own purposes, the Germans concluded, quite illogically, that his story line had also been lifted from *"der heilige N."*

Two generations later, in the 1870s, *Danish* chauvinists attacked the tale, calling it a "brilliant bagatelle" by the young Hans Christian Andersen. The half-Norwegian Norresund obviously could not have penned such a "characteristically Zealandish fable," and that meant that his authorship must be "derivative"—"the competent but uninspired nursing into being of our Copenhagen master's unacknowledged child." That Andersen himself, up to his death in 1875, had never questioned Norresund's authorship, meant little to the "pure Danish" literary elite.

It is regrettable that the world knows Norresund largely through these squabbles, for his tale itself is a delight. The principal character, the "aarborg" Hesperides, must leave the "dry comfort" of its home in the exotic American desert to seek water for its parched family and friends. The search, which takes the form of a classic quest Märchen, brings the creature first to the banks of Old Man River, where it learns the logistical lesson that "you can't carry running water"; then to the Big Rock Candy Mountain, where, with the help of an obliging crow, it secures the blue flower that will serve as the "water key"; and finally back to its sunbaked homeland, where the flower unlocks a water-bursting cactus. The cactus dies, but not before convincing Hesperides to "give back to the earth what you have taken"—and thus ensure the survival of its people.

The mythopoeic delicacy of this tale was appreciated by readers both in Denmark and, after an 1826 translation, in the United States. Sales were not hurt when the American publisher, anticipating modern advertising gimmicks, offered a fifty-dollar prize to the child who could produce the most "believable likeness" of the web-footed, furry aarborg. (The winner, incidentally, was Donald Mapes, the first cousin of Philadelphian Mary Mapes, who forty years later wrote *Hans Brinker*.) The somewhat stodgy American translation has contributed to the story's neglect since that time; so it is with happy expectation that one awaits the revision now being prepared at Oxnard Press.

Tears of Phidias (1823)

Kostas Kostiades

The literature of protest against Turkish rule that was occasioned by the Greek war for independence (1821–29) has become widely publicized through translations. This is not the case with Kostiades's call to arms. Its anglophobic sensibility made it unattractive to British publishers, and it was not until 1965 that the work was made available to English readers.

The sculptor Phidias created most of the exquisite bas reliefs that once adorned the frieze of Athens's Parthenon. These classical masterpieces were spirited out of Greece and into the British Museum in the first decade of the nineteenth century by the British ambassador Lord Elgin, and it is Elgin who is the villain of Kostiades's piece. He functions in the narrative as a modern Paris, snatching the "flower of Aegean beauty" away from the Acropolis and thus bringing on, in the writer's lachrymose phrasing, "years of sorrow, years of emptiness, years of rage."

Just as the "might of Danae" gathered behind Agamemnon to rescue Helen from her foreign "captivity," so modern Greeks, Kostiades implored, should fight for the return of the "horribly misnamed" Elgin Marbles by mounting an invasion of Great Britain. With the foppish and acquisitive George IV on the British throne, Kostiades suggested, the retaking of the marbles should prove "little worry for a people who had been forged for three hundred years in the fire of Turkish domination." Only by so doing, he cried out, could the "tears of Phidias" at last be wiped away.

A historian at the University of Athens, Kostiades clearly meant his tract as propaganda rather than program; accusations that he was "inviting Greece's destruction," made by more than one academic rival, grew from envy rather than serious consideration. Yet not all Greeks took the piece as metaphor. The short-lived little magazine *Hellas Kala* (Beautiful Greece) made its entire thrust the return of the "kidnapped tableaux," and at least twice in the 1830s Lord Elgin, comfortably ensconced in his Surrey estate, received death threats written in archaic, rather than modern, Greek. Nor have contemporary attempts to regain the treasure completely forgotten Kostiades's initial call: a 1974 request by the Greek government that the British Museum surrender its famous possessions referred bluntly to "the Kostiades option" as an alternative to peaceful transfer. The museum took no more notice of the threat then than it had a century and a half before, while the Greek press made much of the "spirit of Kostas" as an element of resurgent Greek pride.

Aside from its political import, *Ta Tou Phidiou Dakrua* is interesting from a purely linguistic standpoint. In the debate between the "archaizing" and "modernizing" literati in the Athens of the 1820s, Kostiades was point man for the "oldsters." Yet his tract clearly espouses a modern theme. Hence it functions as a singular instance in Mediterranean literature of what Carvounis has called "propulsive archaism": the use of a long-outdated dialect to describe contemporary, and even future, possibilities.

The River Novel *(1835)*

Marianne and Thérèse Colombard

The Reader's Encyclopedia calls the roman-fleuve "a novel that deals with a set of characters over a long period of years, usually in a series of volumes." Marianne and Thérèse Colombard wrote precisely this type of novel between 1824 and 1832; it is a sign of the Brontë cult's power that their achievement has been overlooked, and that as perspicacious an editor as William Rose Benét could suppose that "fleuve" suggests the motion of a stream. In fact the original "river" novel (preceding Proust and even Balzac) was called, quite bluntly, *Le Roman Fleuve*, because it told the story of the Fleuve ("River") family, unfolding over a hundred years.

The cast of characters in the Colombards' seven-volume series is a broad and frequently unusual one (see Appendix G for a sampling). From the sixteenth-century patriarch of the Fleuve clan, the one-eyed Gascon carpenter Jules (introduced in the opening volume, *Attention les doigts*, or "Watch Your Fingers"), to the self-styled "clairvoyant banker" Jean-Paul-François (from the final volume *Attention les sous*, or "Watch Your Purse"), the Fleuve family displays a range of perspectives which, in the wry phrasing of Captivus O'Donnelly, "would make a lens grinder go mad." There is more than a novelistic design to this variety, for the Colombard sisters were "vision fanatics" (to adopt the unkind characterization of Brontë apologist Theophilus Duhl): their characters represent not only French social types, but also such alternate perspectives on the human experience as "benevolent sadism," fruititarianism, and phrenology.

The running motif of the enterprise—through almost half a million words of limpid prose—is the nature of perspective, or "variegated vision." The sisters experimented with this motif in several ways that anticipated twentieth-century fiction techniques. Stream of consciousness, jargon, and "mad" speech hint at the provisionality of "common" perception. The third volume—to take only the most glaring example—is narrated by Bérénice Fleuve, a washerwoman who thinks she is a fly.

Feminist scholar Troy Donahue's recent study of the Colombards, *They Were Expendable*, demonstrates why the inventive work of these two women was neglected for so long. At the 1869 International Convocation of Literary Critics, held in London, a proposal was put before the Central Presidium to accept a woman author as an honorary member on the all-male Roll of Classic Writers. The chief contenders were the Colombards and Emily Brontë, and after the company "hooted down" the suggestion that all three women might be included, bitter lobbying erupted. The vocal Brontë forces prevailed, *Wuthering Heights* was deemed acceptable, and the Colombards' work was voted down. One judge went so far as to call the Fleuve cycle "too froggy-minded for anybody's taste. Unless, of course, you're Marcel Proust—and he won't be born for two years."

The Maid Has Left (1838)

Hans Langweiler

German literature in the first half of the nineteenth century was characterized by two contradictory strains: the effusive, often sentimental idealism of "Faust Romantics" and the vociferously bland stoicism of the Biedermeier writers, who saw the striving of the Faustians as ungentlemanly. Hans Langweiler's novel *Das Dienstmädchen Hat den Koop Geflieht* bridged these two sensibilities. His characters are as intense in their passions as any misty-eyed Romantic, yet what they are most intense *about* is their furniture.

The action of the book takes place during one week of "feverish activity" in the home of Johann Stock, a prosperous merchant whose domestic routine has been dealt a body blow by the sudden departure of Flicka, the family maid. Can Flicka be persuaded to return before the weekend, when the Stocks are hosting a Wurstfest for the burgomaster's cousin? If she cannot be persuaded, can Frau Stock find a suitable replacement—one who will not "embarrass us by curtsying too low or polishing the silver with her saliva?" Most important, will the new dining set arrive in time, or will the Stocks be "reduced to the status of Swabians" by having to eat, once again, on hundred-year-old chairs? These are the questions that torment the central characters and that make the novel what one reader has called "a nightmarish exploration of the servant problem."

In his calm, loving appraisal of German domesticity, Langweiler showed a bourgeois self-assurance that was unusually brazen even for a Biedermeier writer. At the same time, the interior monologues of Johann and his wife Gertrude, full of wan despair, showed that the "day-to-day German" could care as deeply as any poet— if he had something to care about. The subtlety was not lost on Langweiler's contemporaries. Adalbert Stifter—renowned for his subtle observation that "a teakettle is as interesting as a volcano"—praised The Maid Has Left as a model of Schicklichkeit, or propriety, and, in one of the more pointed Biedermeier snaps at the Romantics, as ein auf den Linsen der Sternguckere Staubkaninchen, or "a dust bunny on the stargazers' lenses."

Later readers have also responded to the sophistications of this quintessential "novel of table manners." Brunhilde Hapsburg-Beobachten, often referred to as the German Emily Post, considered the book indispensable to a "first-class burgher education." And Boop and Tillyard, in their seminal study of the domestic novel The Hearth of the Matter, say that "by contrast to Langweiler, Jane Austen was a social climber."

A recent dramatization of the book, however, failed badly, when a chic New York playwright, Darcy Precious, attempted to see humor in the Stocks' predicament and to turn their honest anguish into laughter. His play *It's Hard to Get Help in a Hurry* was met with critical sneers and empty houses. "Exactly what he deserved," sniffed the *Times*. "There's nothing funny about spots on the stemware."

Mahoney the Purist *(1841)*

Patrick Meagher

Meagher was a hack writer for a London newspaper when he conceived this strange mixture of politics and mysticism. It is the story of Daniel Mahoney, an Irish worker who digs graves in a London cemetery and whose job, as he tells his wife, is "blissful penance." Penance for *what* is unclear, since Mahoney seems a practically spotless soul, his only vice a Saturday-night "carouse" where, with ritualistic solemnity, he drinks a half pint of stout for every body whose grave he has dug in that week. The first third of the novel shows Mahoney's "purity" even in the act of becoming tipsy, and expresses Meagher's conviction that—as his hero has it—"it hain't what ye do, but 'ow ye do it, what makes ye a 'appy man or a bleedin' fool." The gravedigger's dedication to his much-mocked occupation suggests a religious sophistication that has been called both Christlike and "quasi-Buddhist."

It's true that the novel is contemplative, and Mahoney a sage with a shovel. But it's too simple to reduce the book, as Parker Teakettle has done in a recent essay, to "a game of Zen in the art of shifting dirt." For Mahoney also has a political bent. The fundamental conflict of the novel, in fact, is between his commitment to his work as a kind of moving meditation and his belief in the "righteousness" of appointed authority. His orderly if grubby world is disrupted when three British soldiers are found murdered, and he is told that in the interests of time their graves will be dug not by hand but by a newly purchased steam shovel. "You'll be running this dandy job yourself soon, Danny," the cemetery administrator announces proudly. But Mahoney cannot go along. "If the good Lord had wanted to save us time," he tells his bewildered boss, "He'd of not given us threescore years and ten."

When the administration insists on the machinery, Mahoney pours dirt in its boiler, causing it to malfunction, then digs the three graves by hand, "as yer worship, and the Lord, first intended." Charged with vandalism, he flees the country before his trial and ends up west of Boston on a religious commune. "Me Betsy and me are right happy here," he writes to his brother back in Galway. "Suds, spuds, and no machines."

Meagher's novel has been variously interpreted: as a religious work, as a political protest, as a Rousseauistic paean to the primitive—even as a reworking of the Antigone story. The most fruitful analysis is Russell Thatcher's. In his book *From Micks to Big Macs: Gaelic Threads in Everyday Life*, he paints Mahoney as a "late-blooming Luddite," smashing machinery partly in self-defense, partly as an "endorsement of traditional ways." At the same time, "this Danny boy is a secret patriot: for what Irishman would surrender to a machine the supreme pleasure of digging British graves?"

Six Years with a Donkey (1845)

Myra Quinn

Quinn was the daughter of an eggbeater designer and a folk healer known as the "Mushroom Queen of the Alleghenies." With this background, one might have expected eccentric behavior, and her life does not disappoint that expectation. She left her Philadelphia home in 1829, when she was sixteen, to explore the forests of the southern Appalachians, which had nurtured recently elected president Andrew Jackson. A strong Jacksonian, she went south, as she put it, "to breathe the air and drink the water that had borne a giant." But within a couple of years, she was disillusioned, and became more and more a "renegade to this sorry nation." The story of her "sad education" is told in *Six Years with a Donkey*.

The "Donkey" of the title was actually Thonkeya, a Cherokee Indian whom Quinn met in 1832 and whose people, throughout the 1830s, were being systematically driven from their lands with Jackson's blessings. Quinn traveled with Thonkeya until 1838, when the last of the Cherokee took the infamous Trail of Tears to Oklahoma and Quinn moved to Washington, D.C., to lobby for their relief. The publication of *Six Years* in 1845 was an element of her ongoing outrage.

Not that the book was all politics. Indeed, the brief popularity it enjoyed came about in spite of its "message," and could be traced to its oddball cast of characters. In the duo's six years in the woods, they encountered such "rustic originals" as the three-hundred-pound "white witch" Big Mama Thornton, who invented both Smoky Mountain stew and the mojo hand; the professional story-teller Musgrave "Davy" Cricket, who claimed descent from an alligator and a bear; and the infamous Kallikak Boys of the Georgia highlands, moonshine purveyors who were said to have introduced both drunkenness and cannibalism to the Chickasaw. Quinn and Thonkeya's desperate attempts to mute the effects of such desperadoes, and to restore the supposed "harmonious arrangements" of former days, lend their picaresque adventures a sparse, wan quality that led Thoreau to call the volume "a kind of *Don Quixote* without the quibbling."

As engaging as the travelogue was, its deeper message was not attractive to James Polk's America, which in 1845, following the star of Manifest Destiny, was eyeing Mexican land as it had once eyed Thonkeya's. The first edition of *Six Years*, in fact, omitted Quinn's scathing final chapter, where she likened the displacement of the Five Civilized Tribes to the "overrunning of mighty

Rome by Goths with cravats." The chapter did appear in an 1886 reprint—ironically, just one year before the Dawes Act dealt a death blow to tribal sovereignty.

Quinn died in 1871, after twenty-five years of being known as "the savages' harpy." Thonkeya fell from view in 1838, and is assumed to have entered the Smoky Mountains with those few Cherokee who had avoided the Trail of Tears and whose descendants now live in the Carolinas. Scarlett Biter's suggestion that these Eastern Cherokee are descended from Quinn is, given her lifelong devotion to celibacy, a contemptible canard.

The Flower Seller *(1851)*

Gaston Courbet

Overshadowed by his painter brother Gustave for a century, Gaston Courbet is now enjoying a posthumous celebrity following a reassessment of his work in the 1960s which concluded he had influenced Flaubert. It seems unfortunate, if predictable, to have his name thus tacked on again to a "greater" figure's, for his finest novel, *La Vendeuse des fleurs*, is as accomplished as anything in its period.

Like his brother, Gaston was a realist with an affection for the minor details of mundane life. Gustave's famous definition of painting as "nothing more than the representation of real and concrete things" is as applicable to Gaston's literary works as to those his brother put on canvas; with characteristic modesty, he once proclaimed himself the Pack Rat of Paris, "picking up a shred here, a button there, to show you, honored Reader, the nest of life."

In *La Vendeuse*, he displayed that portion of the "nest" that lined the Seine between the old Hôtel de Ville and the Place des Vosges—in his day the center of public life. His narrator is an aged flower seller, Madame Elise, who from her "pitch" outside the steps of the city hall is able to observe "the high and the low and the caught-between" as they "pass through the gate, and go away, and pass through again." As visitors and dignitaries come and go, Madame gives us not only quite "painterly" details of dress and appearance, but also a running commentary on their private lives. So acute an eye does Courbet give his narrator that in the amalgamation of her myriad snapshots, we get a rich, organic tableau of Parisian life.

Madame's depictions of obscure city folk are exceptionally sharp. We have Monsieur Varenne, for example, a tax official who each Friday buys one "rose of appeasement" for the wife he will be cheating on that afternoon. Little Mariane, the kosher butcher's daughter from the nearby Marais, who in sabots and Breton clothing delivers chops to anti-Semitic government officers. And the Beauregard sisters, proprietors of a local bistro who smell like goose fat, wear red scarves to advertise their socialist sympathies, and are so grossly mismatched in size that Madame calls them *Le Muid* (the hogshead) and *L' Epingle* (the pin).

But Courbet does not spare the famous. His book is no roman à clef, to be sure, but it does contain memorable portraits of the mighty. From her vantage point outside city hall, Madame witnesses Lamartine's exhortation to the crowd during the Revolution of 1848, and she reveals her own radical sympathies when she observes, "The people asked him to speak about bread. The poet wrapped himself in the tricolor and smiled broadly." This novel is also the first place in literature where the "banker king" Louis Philippe appears with his iconographic tag, a black umbrella.

The influence on Flaubert would be obvious even if the master himself had not spelled it out. Flaubert acknowledges in a letter that remained unpublished until 1961, that Hugo was his "god," but that his style—the precise accumulation of telling details—was his personal "*hommage à GC.*" It is a comment on the inertia of received wisdom that, before they reconsidered *La Vendeuse*, most scholars thought he meant the painter.

The Urchin Papers *(1859–62)*

Liddell Dickens

When we refer to a troublesome youngster as a "little Dickens," we are recalling the career of Charles Dickens's second cousin, Liddell Pecksniffia Dickens, who both tantalized and infuriated the master's readers in the 1860s with her impertinent "addenda" to his novels. Presented as correctives to his sentimentality about the young, they appeared originally in the London monthly *Blunt's*, under the byline "L.D.," and were collected as *The Urchin Papers* in 1863. *Blunt's* editor Martin Forcemeat aptly described their intent as "de-sugaring, or seeing the brats *as they are*."

The inaugural tale in L.D.'s debunking cycle was "Tommie Twaddle, or the Legpuller's Holiday." In it, the guileless Tommie

Traddle of *David Copperfield* becomes an unctuous master of deceit, responding to the most innocent observations with a sneer and the catchphrase "I *believe* it." The next was the popular "Little Pill," in which the universally adored heroine of *The Old Curiosity Shop*, Little Nell, acquires a fortune as an artist's model and a disposition that would curdle cream: "an accomplished musician," wrote L.D., she knew "seven whines in middle C alone." In "The Spirit of Christmas Once Removed," we find an enterprising teenager named Portly Tim running a charity con game which he defends with his Uncle Screw's favorite maxim: "God helps those who help themselves." And in the 1862 "What Miss Havisham Knew," we find a young cad named Pipsqueak cheating on his wife Stella while a ghostly Miss Havisham admonishes, "I told you he was rotten, you stupid girl."

The snideness of the stories notwithstanding, they may have carried a hidden message of reform. As Chauncey Pestergrove explained in his classic essay "Big Dickens and Little Dickens," the "very fact that Pipsqueak was a bounder encouraged fidelity in an increasingly faithless age," while Portly Tim's smugness was "less an inducement toward, than a warning against, the mercenary venality he exhibited."

Possibly, then, it was the stories' "idealism" that kept Charles from denouncing his cousin. Constantly urged to sue her for libel, he kept silent but for one ambiguous utterance. When asked to comment on the L.D. vogue at an 1861 lecture, he said, "I suppose there's a little pill in us all." Literary revisionists have taken this as proof of the master's suppressed "dark vision" of prepubescence, although there is a simpler, economic explanation—that Dickens realized the spoofs boosted his sales. After the 1861 appearance of "Twisted Ollie," for example, a reprint of the 1839 *Oliver Twist* sold out in only two months.

Aside from the term "Liddell Dickens," the L.D. affair had another legacy. The American version of a Liddell Dickens character was the less corrupt but still mischievous Peck's Bad Boy. His creator, journalist George Peck, acknowledged in his 1913 autobiography that he had modeled his youthful prankster on "L.D.'s brats—as endearing a pack of scamps as ever broke a window. Encountering them in my youth was a breath of air, for, to tell the truth, Nell made me ill."

Zigismondo's Dogpipe (1863)

Antonio Ghirardelli

The father of Italian verismo, Giovanni Verga, called this delightful glimpse into the customs of rural Malta "a definitive influence on my own writing," and Maltese critic Alqaq Sanguarancia goes even further: "Without *Il zagg di Zigismondo*, there would have been no naturalistic novel; Verga's entire shtick was born on Gozo."

Even making allowances for Sanguarancia's chauvinism, his fellow Maltese's novel is a stunning work. In a fascinating mélange of Arabic, Italian, and local dialects, it tells the story of the goatherd Zigismondo Tal, who leaves his farm at the age of twenty-one to wander the roads of his native island as a musician. His instrument, the native *zagg*, or "dogpipe," resembles the bagpipe except that the bag is an inflated dogskin and the "pipes" are the animal's extended legs. With "tamba" players Filfla and Comino, Zigismondo becomes a local hero, not only because of his "Orphean magic," but because, in his zeal to preserve the island's culture, he defends its ways against English detractors.

Malta was part of the British Empire in 1863, and the dramatic focus of Ghirardelli's novel is the attempt by the island's rigid governor, Sir Horatio Frumm, to ban the traditional *festivale de carrobia*, or carob festival. During this weeklong celebration, revelers consume huge quantities of carob-laced "Malta milk," smear their bodies with carob paste, and dance around the clock to praise Carobia, the pagan fertility goddess who, legend says, brought the plant to the island. Frumm wants it outlawed on the grounds that it is "sensually stimulating and therefore anti-British." Zigismondo and his companions champion its preservation, becoming *brigands bien-aimés* when they pelt the governor's mansion with carob pods, publicly perform the outlawed "Hymns to Carobia," and even create a new dance in her honor. They call it, appropriately enough, the Ziggy Zagg; the twitted Frumm moans that it resembles "the erratic skips and hops of a wild Comanche."

A rapprochement is achieved, ironically, when the musicians are arrested for public indecency. Awaiting trial, they convert their jailers—including Frumm himself—to an appreciation of the "divine pod" by singing the hypnotic aria *"Confetto bruno e dolce"*—whereupon the ban is rescinded and the festivities proceed. In one of those small touches of sentiment that Ghirardelli's readers have always admired, it is Filfla, the second *tamburinina*, who is elected carob queen.

The novel was first translated into English in 1878, under the title given here. More fanciful translations came in this century, with the recovery of Italian realism after the Second World War. It was reissued in 1950 as *Zig's Zagg*, and in 1965 as *Devil Dancers of Gozo*—a shameless, and thankfully unsuccessful, bid to tap the satanist health food market.

The obvious family connection between Antonio Ghirardelli of Malta and chocolate magnate Giuseppe Ghirardelli of Milan was never a very happy one. Antonio was a "carobist" to his dying day, and never forgave his successful cousin for "forsaking Carobia for Mammon." The Milan merchant's assessment of Antonio was no kinder. In a slang phrase that has become a typical Milanese taunt, he commented on the success of his cousin's book, *"Tanto Malti, molto tonti,"* or "So Maltese—totally nuts."

Danger and Distance (1874)

Reginald Jeffries

Most observers of the Crimean War concur that the infamous Charge of the Light Brigade, in which over two hundred British soldiers lost their lives because of ludicrous orders by their commanders, was a debacle. Reginald Jeffries, who survived the charge, disagreed. Far from regretting the slaughter, he spent his remaining forty-five years defending October 12, 1854, as the "swan song of all martial honour." So he said in countless addresses, and in his influential memoir *Danger and Distance: or, The Decline of Heroism.*

To Jeffries, martial heroics were the expression of that "essential manly virtue which has sustained the white race from the days of Roland to the present." In a volume that owed as much to Darwin as to Whitehall, Jeffries applauded the "great game" of expansionism as "a fittingly Anglo-Saxon affirmation of noble sacrifice—as invigorating as Thermopylae or Roncevalles." The Jeffries universe, obviously, was not only mystically romantic but staunchly racist as well: his disdain for what Homer Lea called the Slavic swarm was so intense that he referred to Czar Alexander II's freeing of the serfs as a "mongrel Mongol ploy."

Since such sentiments were not unusual at the time, Jeffries might have remained a regimental footnote had *Danger and Distance* not promoted, in addition to the barracks bravado, an ironic program of disarmament. What had sapped the strength of modern peoples, he felt, was not a Spenglerian lack of will, but technology—gimmicks that made possible "anonymous slaughter, slaughter at a distance, the very antithesis of personal combat."

Jeffries condemned modern warfare because it relied inevitably on such gimmicks. The man who considered archery "the beginning of the end for true nobility" could hardly be expected to look favorably on cannon, and he did not; gunpowder he considered "the heathen Chinee's most pernicious invention," and he bridled when his personal hero, the Frankish warrior Roland, was compared to British martyr Charles Gordon—that "popinjay with a handgun."

Such a philosophy was bound to generate queer alliances. In 1863, as the American Civil War was demonstrating the effectiveness of mechanical carnage, Jeffries joined the New Elham Pacifist Society, and soon became one of its most popular speakers. In 1871, after the Franco-Prussian War had ushered the machine gun into the modern arsenal, he wrote vitriolic letters to the *Times* on behalf of a phantom organization called the Pan-European Disarmament League (PEDAL), demanding that Hiram Maxim, the gun's inventor, be banished to the Congo for a thousand years. "There he should be made to eat ants," wrote Jeffries imperiously, "as retribution for having midgetised a noble race."

Danger and Distance enabled Jeffries to buy a farm which he converted into a fencing and riding academy. At his death just before the turn of the century, he was still teaching saber work to British schoolboys, and lamenting modernity in his newsletter *Roland's Horn*. Most military experts thought him a crackpot, but he had friends in high places, and his atavistic outlook contributed to British unreadiness for World War I.

Moose Nose and Other Poems (1875)

Clyde Ormond

Ten years before the birth of his fellow Idahoan Ezra Pound, woodsman Clyde Ormond published a collection of "rustic lyrics" that anticipated Imagism by forty years and that, even among the caustically demanding Boise culture crowd, were an instant (and lasting) hit. Two examples will give the flavor of Ormond's back-woods vision. Here is the beginning of his endearing "Moose Call":

> *Place it over the lips and make a grunting sound,*
> *Uh-waugh! Uh-waugh!*
> *Expelling lungfuls of air helps the effort.*
> *It resembles the love call of a moose*
> *And it will carry for miles.*

By way of contrast to this free, Whitmanesque exercise, here is his less characteristic, but no less surefooted, management of traditional seven-foot unrhymed couplets in the lovingly detailed "Grub":

> *Butter or syrup, jelly or jam,*
> *Are normally used on hotcakes.*
> *One ounce of butter is certainly ample*
> *And three of the syrup will do.*

As a final example of the broad palette that this son of the Bitteroot Range liked to use, consider the short piece that won him the Thoreau Prize in 1874, "Estimating Bird Flocks":

> *Count a group of ten.*
> *See about how many groups*
> *There are. Multiply.*

The attentive reader will notice that this poem elegantly observes the strict format of the so-called "American haiku" or "math-ku," in that its obligatory seventeen syllables "refract" the traditional Japanese nature images by the subtle intrusion of mathematics. It was this second stylistic similarity to Pound that led the *Poetry Unbound* staff in 1928 to mount an expedition to the environs of Boise, to determine whether something in the Idaho air or water might have contributed to the rise of Imagism.

The expedition was inconclusive and, in the words of then ex-

patriated Pound (who heard about it from Monroe Harry), "as outlandish a squandering of artistic energies as the West has seen
since doddering Wordsworth died." The far more modest Ormond,
then ninety-seven, also pooh-poohed the investigation, though with
better manners: his note thanking Monroe for her interest in "potato country" offered "sympathy with your endeavors: I once tried
to buttonhole a deer myself."

Unlike other regional writers, Ormond never became known
outside of his region. He couldn't have cared less. He raised sheep,
hunted, fished, and generally enjoyed himself, as he put it, "every
day that the good Lord give me." When he lay dying in 1929,
some months short of one hundred, he expressed only one re-
gret: "If I'd a made it to the big three, it'da made a damn good
math-ku."

Oskar Tschirsky (1875)

Mikhail Gormandov

A luxuriously deliquescent Russian novel, this small masterpiece by the "playboy philosopher" Gormandov chronicles the rise and fall of the White Russian chef Oskar Tschirsky from the slums of imperial Moscow to the tables of New York's fabled 400 and back again. A worldly, literate Bildungsroman, it fascinated its original audience of middle-class readers by providing detailed programs for becoming nouveau gauche; today it is valuable primarily for the light it casts on Gilded Age social values.

Tschirsky is a Moscow-bred "rat man"—an official poisoner of the city's vermin—who leaves his homeland at twenty to make his fortune. He goes first to Paris, where he learns cooking under the redoubtable Escoffier; then, as a *saucier*, he travels to New York, where he excels as a chef on Millionaire's Row: among the celebrities that Gormandov has him cook for are the Astors, the J. P. Morgans, and the John D. Rockefellers; among the dishes he is credited with creating for this luminous clientele are oysters Rockefeller, veal Oscar, and White Russian pizza. He is also seen as something of a revolutionary in his attempts to introduce salad to carnivorous America; his explanation of roughage to a bewildered John Delmonico is, in the words of Carlos Fryer, "one of the most heart wrenching scenes in all literature."

His culinary daring eventually proves his undoing, for in recommending honey as a sweetener, he runs afoul of the powerful Sugar Trust, and is forced to leave town under a cloud. The novel ends with him, broken in spirit, back with the Moscow Vermin Brigade, consoling himself with the bitter knowledge that "at least these rats know what they are."

Discursive in parts, and occasionally freighted with unnecessary gastronomic detail, the novel at its best is a breezy account not only of a peculiar education, but also of glitterati life-styles in the

Seamy Sixties. Gormandov, a former roving correspondent for *Caviar Weekly*, was both attracted to and repelled by the haut monde, and his ambivalence shows: his "banquet on horseback" is a satirical plum, as is the characterization of society doyenne Mrs. Ward McAllister as "a goose wearing pearls."

Missing his satire, Gormandov's targets took his novel as prescriptive. The New York Athletic Club thought his concept of an "equine extravaganza" just the ticket—and mounted one itself in 1880. By that year, too, every fancy restaurant in New York had placed veal Oscar on the menu. And a Gormandov countryman, baker Shem Raskolnikov, made *his* fortune in cuisine by adopting the name "Oscar Tschirsky" and becoming chef at the Waldorf-Astoria. This odd case of life imitating art is described in Fryer's book *Oscar Real and Veal*; Fryer also provides the definitive catalog of variants on Tschirsky's most famous creation—including recipes for veal pseudo-Oscar and (Fryer's personal favorite) Oscar poi.

The Lost Art of Cow-Tipping *(1879)*

Joel Furlow

"There is nothing so inspiring on a drunken evening as the sight of a sleeping Hampshire cow." So begins the poignant "instructional memoir" that gave journalist Joel Furlow his fame. Born in tiny Thornton's Ferry, New Hampshire, Furlow grew up on a dairy farm just as "those twin Leviathans," the textile and railroad industries, were beginning to carve away unremittingly at the rural landscape. *Cow-Tipping*, like most of his other works, was a chatty, elegiac look at passing ways which contained a fair portion of venom for city slickers. An instant hit, it saw ten printings before World War I, establishing its author as New Hampshire's major rural voice at just the time when the state was becoming "cosmopolized" (to use his term) by money interests from Manchester and Boston.

In Furlow's youth the Granite State was known as "Cowhampshire," both among tittering "Southerners" (Furlow's term for Bay Staters and the "rabble beyond") and among New Hampshire natives themselves. Until the 1830s, cattle were a way of life: "all of our business, and most of our pleasure, involved the cow." Among the pleasures was the post-tavern entertainment known as "bossy-stalking" or "cow-tipping." This involved sneaking up on a sleeping animal (like horses, cattle can sleep on their feet) and pushing it over onto its side. It was around tales of this piquant diversion that Furlow wove the tapestry of rural life that gave him the sobriquet "Hamp's Thoreau."

"The hazards of the enterprise [wrote Furlow] are principally two: that the heifer will start before you do, and thus escape; or that she will fall wrong, like a poorly notched pine, and flatten you. Along the Suncook River this is known as 'pancaking,' and I have known of only one pancake to survive. A night of tipping is thus no faintheart's frolic, but an adventure where only the stalwart may sound their horns."

Much of the book is devoted to reminiscences of the author's own tipping escapades, but there are also obiter dicta about White Mountain folkways in the 1800s. Neville Chuck, author of the prizewinning study *The Cow in Cross-Cultural Context*, calls Fur-

low's work "absolutely essential for an understanding of New England boviana." Furlow's book includes, for example, a comparison of New England tanning techniques, the definitive milk-production statistics for the Suncook *and* Soucook river valleys, and a recipe for "Cheshire County cow patty" which even Utah Phillips, long scornful of beef delicacies, admits "compares very favorably with moose-turd pie."

Furlow was the nephew and namesake of Joel Barlow, the colonial-era Connecticut Wit. He changed his name to establish his own reputation, "rather than steal coattail celebrity," and to distance himself from "them townie twits." This was entirely in character for a man who called Connecticut "Massachusetts's sour udder," and who ran for Congress on a reform platform in 1880, claiming that "no man who cannot milk a cow should have the chance to milk the public purse."

Furlow's other books were *Live Free or Die* (1873), whose title New Hampshire adopted as its state motto, and *Slickerism Redefined* (1876), a vigorous denunciation of his bête noire, the Connecticut Yankee.

The Rubaiyat of
Omar Khayyam *(12th Century)*

Translated by Alexander Yarrowville (1884)

For over a century, the names Omar Khayyam and Edward Fitzgerald have been as inseparably linked as those of Gilbert and Sullivan or Pregfoot and Barenant. To most English-speaking readers, the fatalistic verve of the Persian poet is known only through the Fitzgerald translation, and the idea that someone other than "dear old Fitz" (as Tennyson called him) might do the quatrains better justice has always struck *Rubaiyat* lovers as outlandish. The consensus remains with Yale orientalist P. V. Palfrey, who, in a stinging analysis of "Rubaiyat revisionism," called the desire for an improved translation evidence of "dementia Baconiensis." Writing in *Acta Orientalia* in 1884, he proclaimed, *Non fracta res non restituenda est*, or "If it ain't broke, don't fix it."

This snap was directed at Palfrey's scholarly rival Alexander Yarrowville, who had just published a "colloquial" version of the quatrains in the avowedly "antiliterary" *Boston Phoenix*. Appointed the youngest-ever member of Harvard's Oriental Studies faculty in 1870, Yarrowville had first ruffled Palfrey's feathers two years earlier in calling his study of links between Tibetan lamaism and Roman Catholicism "a fine mist of Eurocentric piffle." Palfrey had defended himself in the celebrated monograph *Lhasa: the Fourth Rome*, and the battle was then forever joined. For over two decades the Yarrowville-Palfrey tiff enlivened debate at Orientalist meetings, becoming in its own sequestered fashion the Pope-Phillips feud of its time.

Even without this background animus, the Yarrowville *Rubaiyat* would have been hard to take. With that passion for the offbeat and the demotic that came to fruition in his *Cockney Street Slang* (1897), he rendered Omar's twelfth-century Persian into a modern equivalent of "tentmakers' slang"—avoiding the "poetified niceties" of Fitzgerald on the one hand and the "more intelligible banalities of Mr. Whinfield" on the other.* The result was a curious confection whose queer energy is best seen in comparison. Here, for example, is Fitzgerald's famous first quatrain:

> *Awake! for Morning in the Bowl of Night*
> *Has flung the Stone that puts the Stars to Flight:*
> *And Lo! the Hunter of the East has caught*
> *The Sultan's Turret in a Noose of Light.*

---

* Brace Whinfield published a bland, entirely respectable translation in 1847.

Here is the Yarrowville version:

> Get up! you sluggard, and take them reins
> Your nag is ready to run.
> That poker you feel stirring your brains
> Ain't no poker, boy, it's the sun.

Here is Fitzgerald's moving comment, in Quatrain 51, on the irreversibility of time:

> The Moving Finger writes; and, having writ,
> Moves on: nor all thy Piety nor Wit
> Shall lure it back to cancel half a Line,
> Nor all thy Tears wash out a Word of it.

And here is Yarrowville's rendition:

> If faith can move mountains and beggars can ride,
> I said to a learned old goat,
> Make me twenty again, with my spunk and my grin,
> When the Reaper says, "That's all she wrote."

Finally, the most famous of Fitzgerald's Omarisms, the "wilderness" quatrain, number 11:

> A Book of Verses underneath the Bough,
> A Jug of Wine, a Loaf of Bread—and Thou
> Beside me singing in the Wilderness—
> Oh, Wilderness were Paradise enow!

Yarrowville, with what Palfrey called "indefensible blatancy," captured the erotic hint of that passage in this way:

> If this is a desert it suits me.
> With a bottle, a bun, and a book,
> We can dine on all three, and each other:
> Wasn't that the earth that just shook?

Victorian readers, attuned to the recherché sonorities of dear old Fitz, did not take kindly to such bluntness, and the spurned Yarrowville version was soon forgotten. It enjoyed a brief revival in the 1930s, when the Prole School praised it as a rare example of "English as she is spoke." Forgotten again today, it is nonetheless to be recommended to anyone who feels that Wordsworth may have been on target when he claimed that poetry should eschew the ornate and "imitate, as far as possible, the very language of men."

Leaps and Excavations (1889)

F. T. Antonio-Marcos

The Venezuelan writer Francisco Tomás Antonio-Marcos was, until the publication of this puzzling volume, a conventional historian and archaeologist. While studying philology at the Royal and Pontifical University in Mexico City, he became fascinated by the discovery of Mayan ruins in the Yucatan interior, and turned with a passion to prehistory. Between 1850 and 1880, as a professor at various universities, he published widely in archaeological journals, establishing a reputation in Mesoamerican dating. Sometime after 1880, however, while on a dig in central Mexico, he underwent what he described as a "radical reassessment vision" and what his colleagues saw, variously, as a peyote-induced hallucination or senility. The book that came out of this experience appeared in 1889 as *Saltos y excavaciones*.

Had it been written by anyone but a professional archaeologist, the volume might have been dismissed as mere whimsy. Coming from Antonio-Marcos, it created a storm of controversy, for it depicted the widely accepted prehistoric chronology—Stone Age, Bronze Age, and Iron Age—as "a plausible, but quite unprovable, fancy." *Saltos y excavaciones* was composed of supposed "field sketches" that the author had made on his travels; in the most notorious of these sketches, Antonio-Marcos claimed to have discovered, in a Middle Stone Age site in Guatemala, an aluminum frying pan. His conclusion—hardly designed to endear him to fellow scholars—was that conventional stratigraphy was wrong: the sequence should be Old Stone, Aluminum, New Stone, Bronze, and Iron.

Since European factories had only begun to produce aluminum commercially in the 1860s, Antonio-Marcos's "find" was all the more remarkable. And that wasn't the only shocker he trotted out. In a sketch on the Mayan Well of Sacrifice at Chichén Itzá, he claimed to have found embedded in the bottom mud a "Santa Claus figurine" and a small typewriter. In "The Icicle of Cholula," he described a subterranean cavern hung not with conventional limestone stalactites, but with "coolly dripping, aqueous versions of the same, many of them tasting of sarsaparilla." And in "Pieces of Sky," he speculated that certain clay fragments, known to the Olmecs as "sky drops," were vestiges of the legendary "Pitcher of Heaven" mentioned in folklore as the source of rain.

No fellow archaeologist took this seriously, and Antonio-Marcos, after a couple of years trying to gain converts, disappeared into the Yucatan jungle, where, he promised, he would "find the one piece of proof that cannot be denied." Since he never defined what he meant by this, and since he never returned, his book quickly dropped from public view, and Mesoamericanists chuckled to each other that the world was well rid of another crackpot. Only in the 1980s, with antiuniformitarianism again on the rise, have his sketches come into their own. Frederick Catherwood's centennial translation of *Saltos y excavaciones*, just issued by the Cenote Press, has begun to restore its author's dignity, and there is even a Caracas movement afoot to make Antonio-Marcos, posthumously, the national archaeologist of Venezuela.

My Wildest Trip (1897)

Maturin M. Ballou

A co-founder and first editor of the *Boston Globe*, Ballou left desk-bound journalism in 1875 to spend the latter half of his life seeing the world. A tireless traveler with an eye for detail, he produced over a dozen entertaining travel memoirs, bringing his readers to such far-flung locations as Central America, Alaska, and Australia.

None of his books was more entertaining than the journal of his last trip, to the land he called Ultima Thule. Fascinated by polar climates, Ballou had made several journeys past the Arctic Circle, and had enjoyed considerable success with his "glimpse of Lappish life," *Far North*. To follow up on this success, he determined in 1894 to "travel as near to the North Pole as reason allows, to breathe the pure, crackling air of the Great Silence." He chose his words only too well, for in spite of his concessions to "reason," this polar trek was to prove his undoing: he never lived to see his journal published.

To the ancient Romans, Thule was an island six days' sail north of Britain, and the expression "ultima Thule" meant, roughly, "the ends of the earth." It's still an accurate description of the Poles, and in 1897 it was even more apt, for neither one had yet been reached; the closest stab was made in 1895, by the seasoned Arctic trekkers Nansen and Johansen; for a tenderfoot like Ballou, used to the satin sheets of grand hotels, to undertake such a journey was, in the words of his sister Sophie, "proof positive that Matty had gone batty."

My Wildest Trip provided plenty of evidence that her assessment might have been right, for the style was uncharacteristically weird. Here, for example, is Ballou writing in 1893, on the desert regions of Down Under: "It was formerly thought that the dry, cracked soil of the Australian pampas was nearer to positive sterility than that of any known region." Compare that luxuriant periodicity with the clipped, strobelike description of northern Greenland: "Green, what? You say. Blank. All blank, and a chilly one, too. What mules we fardels be, white white white. Is it not true? What *do* they say of the reindeer girls?"

What James Leach calls the "erratic-ecstatic" tone of such passages (and there are many in the book) has been seen as evidence of many possible afflictions, ranging from salmonella poisoning (the so-called tainted-reindeer-meat theory) to oversensitivity to the Northern Lights to simple drunkenness. Whatever the reason, Ballou's record is extraordinarily discombobulated for a person of his journalistic skills—so much so that the slang expression "tripping," for undertaking a visionary, often drug-induced quest, has been traced to his curiously puerile title.

The most extraordinary feature of the journal, however, was not the style but the author's fateful encounter with the "Skraelings," a "lost tribe" of seven-foot, fur-clad "power wizards" who lived, they told Ballou, at the center of the earth. He describes their "interior city" in fitful sketches—there is much talk of swastika-shaped buildings and "polar power"—and then, in a passage that tantalized as well as frustrated many readers, he takes leave of

"the outer world" to join his new companions: "These scribblings be my testament," he concludes. "The Skraemobile awaits and I descend. Last trip, greatest trip. Kiss the kids." (The fact that Ballou had no children added to his readers' consternation.)

Ballou's journal was discovered in 1909 by the more successful Peary expedition. His remains have never been found, which has led the more credulous of readers to suppose that "Skraelingland" really did (or does) exist. The Tennessee-based Hollow Earth Society even takes *My Greatest Trip* as its sacred text, and has pestered the Department of the Interior for years for a grant to follow Ballou "down the hole." "We have every expectation," Society President Floyd Oversight told me recently, "that if Star Wars can get money, we can too."

The Vicarage (1901)

Eden Philpotts

Eden Philpotts, often called the Devonshire Hardy, wrote six novels of English rural life. Most of them deserve their oblivion, but *The Vicarage* merits a closer scrutiny because of its influence on this century's major poet. T. S. Eliot was never man enough to own up to it, but his debt to the minor novelist is unmistakable: not only the title, but the plan and a good deal of the incidental symbolism of his poem "Prufrock" were suggested by the Devon writer's volume.

The novel's protagonist is J. Alfred Testpater, a "malignantly reflective" country vicar who suffers not only from theological doubts, but also from physical obsessions ranging from the sexual to the meteorological: among the "manifestations of God's prolixity" that cause him concern are thunderstorms, stray dogs, peaches, Romanesque architecture, and his own feet. The ingenious Noah Flagrant spots a pattern here. "The cleric is fascinated and repelled by sheer anomaly," he says. "What does not fit tries his Anglican soul, and so he is guiltily titillated by the irregular ('loose' beasts, 'hairy' fruit), the transcendent (rough weather, sublime buildings), and the forbidden (foot fetishism was rampant in Philpotts's day)."

If Flagrant is right, and I think he is, we might read the novel as an allegorical "trial"—not only of the hapless cleric himself, but of the antilatitudinarianism that he uncomfortably espouses. The name Testpater is hardly accidental, for the novel is a testing of the Father (Latin *pater*) and of his church, founded on a rock (Greek *petros*). The theme is most poignantly explored in a dialogue between Testpater and his daughter Hope, when the girl asks, "If God sees every sparrow fall, why doesn't he catch more before they're mush?"

The Vicarage went on the Great Books list at Harvard College two years before Eliot matriculated, and it is clear that he borrowed from it heavily in composing the poem that made his reputation. Prufrock (prove-rock) *is* Testpater, with all his politesse and indecision. He wears, like the vicar, white flannel trousers; the vicar wears them rolled up, to see his feet. Testpater once "dares to eat a peach"—and suffers dizzying remorse as a result. And in the novel, as in the poem, the hero is confounded by yakking aesthetes: "I am so tired of hearing about painting," Testpater complains to his wife. "And who is this wog Michael Angel?"

It may not be too sweeping a generalization to suggest that Eliot's entire oeuvre was a "pater-testing," and if that is so, credit Philpotts. "Whole volumes have been penned on Jessie Weston," critic Janet Slythe once rightly complained. "Surely the muse for 'Prufrock' deserves as much?"

My True Story (1902)

Robert Wire

This "authentic account of life in the Old West" starts by placing the eastern border of that fabled territory "neither in Texas nor in Tombstone," but in White House Station, New Jersey. Wire describes it as a rough-and-tumble hamlet just east of the Delaware Water Gap where he was "borned, raised up, and larnt to bronco-bust by a woman what made Calamity Jane look like Lady Astor." The woman was his mother, Pistol Patty. A former dance-hall queen from the "hell town of South Bound Brook," she could "outshoot Annie Oakley, outeat Diamond Jim Brady, and whup any man short of Gentleman Jim."

Determined to groom her son for a theatrical career, Patty taught him to ride bareback by the age of two and to "do handstands on galloping stallions afore I could spit." Armed with this arcane skill, Wire joined Buffalo Bill's Wild West extravaganza in 1891, but he soon proved "too wild for them Dakota pantywaists" and was let go after one season. After roaming the Canadian high plains for several years, he returned to White House Station around 1900, opened a dude ranch called the Tin Pony, and regaled visitors with tales of his exploits—duly recorded two years later in *My True Story*.

The exploits included such obvious Pecos Bill thefts as riding a tornado, pulling a mountain lion inside out, and lassoing the moon. But Wire did have wonders of his own. In desolate Saskatchewan, he wrote, he eluded a band of scalp-hungry Cree by leaping into the air behind a cloud. In Manitoba, confronted by a river so cold that "youda froze solid if you forded it," he "hoisted the troubling tributary by its own petard and waltzed my way, lickety-split, under it." And in his home state of New Jersey, harassed by the notorious Secaucus Seven gang, he leveled the entire bunch with one blow, punching the leader so hard that his violent staggers knocked out the rest.

Because Wire never knew his father, and because certain evidence points to Ned Buntline, it has been said that his story was meant as a slap at the famous dime novelist—a reductio ad absurdum of the Cody-Carson pulp genre that both copied and ridiculed his absent parent. A less psychoanalytical reading would place *My True Story* in the tall-tale tradition: Tyler Keogh calls it a "perfect type of modern fakelore."

Whichever interpretation is correct, there is no doubting the Wire book's appeal: between 1902 and the First World War, it was reprinted more times than any "western" book but Wister's *Virginian*. In that same period, sporting a ten-inch handlebar mustache and an armadillo shell for a hat, Wire was a favorite on the lecture circuit, where he milked his *True Story* persona to the limit. He made enough on royalties and lecture fees to give up the Tin Pony in 1910 and move Patty and himself to sedate New Brunswick, where he lived until his death in 1921.

As Keogh reveals in his coolly nostalgic triple portrait *Two Bills and a Bob: the Lives of Bronco Billy, William S. Hart, and Robert Wire* (1934), Wire also modestly influenced American film. Not only was *The Great Train Robbery* filmed on his New Jersey property, but he himself played the outlaw leader who ends the landmark film by shooting the camera.

A Reader's Journal (1907–16)

Milton St. John

While he was an undergraduate at Yale, St. John was told by a revered professor that his "reverse namesake" John Milton had been the last person alive to have read everything ever written. Already aghast at the responsibility of carrying the Puritan giant's name around ("even palindromically," he said), St. John took this revelation as a personal challenge and decided that, before he died, he would duplicate Milton's feat.

With one emendation, however. Even the eccentric St. John was not so deluded as to suppose that the modern world's blizzard of verbiage was accessible to a single soul. So he determined to read only material that had been published after Milton's death ("My progenitor [sic]," he explained, "has already covered that stuff.") And in a further nod to modesty, he decided not to attempt "every backwater poetaster's trivialities," but to concentrate on the "Great Works"—those masterpieces of literary style or philosophical cogency that had "earned a place at the Muses' select table."

Taking as the Muses' checklist the 1894 *Encyclopedia of World Literature*, St. John began methodically with the *A*'s, hoping—as he said in his first journal entry—"to make it to Zola before I die." Being unburdened by financial worries (he was the great-nephew of industrialist Augustus Boyne) and blessed with a talent for languages, he set to work in the spring of 1907, "looking forward to the great Aeschylus and Augustine but discovering, before three days were out, that I had first to overcome a Danish hurdle." That hurdle, of course, was *Children of Wrath*, the phenomenal first novel by Jeppe Aakjaer, which had taken the literary world by storm two years earlier. It took St. John months of his schedule, he tells us dolefully, "to even begin to understand the Danish optative," and as a result his *magnum opus legendum* was "stalled in the gate for two years."

When he got out of the gate, and had zipped through Ivar Aasen in short order, things went swimmingly for several years. He did Paul Adam's sixteen-volume *Temps de la vie* in six weeks, Aeschylus in less than a month, and Aesop in a week and a half. But then he encountered a second hurdle: the Finnish realist Juhani Aho. In spite of his linguistic gifts, St. John found the twelve cases of classical Finnish "utterly daunting," and was quickly reduced to writing "such monstrous solecisms" as "The fat ball threw the rubber boy."

Aho was to prove St. John's undoing. After five years of "grappling with their bestial subjunctive" and a two-month stint with tutors in Helsinki, he gave up the project as a bad bet and became a professor of Renaissance French in Lyon. To friends who observed that he might have read Aho in translation (the English version of his *Parson's Daughter* had been out since 1863), St. John had an imperious response: "Would the sainted Milton have read Genesis in James's version?"

The story of St. John's wrestling with the "angel of inflection" is told laboriously but charmingly in this multivolume journal. It has been likened to Proust for its irrelevant detail, and in 1951 it was afforded the Helsinki Academy's "Good Try" prize for "that work of literature which most conspicuously demonstrates the richly puzzling aspects of Finnish endings."

The Metab Factor *(1909)*

Bernard Fresh

Had Bernard Fresh lived in the 1970s, he would certainly have achieved fame and fortune, for his magnum opus, *Personality: The Metab Factor*, has all the attributes of a pop-psychology classic. It is crisply written, consistently entertaining, and it reduces all human dynamics to a single variable. Unfortunately, he wrote at a time when depth psychology had so captured the public imagination that non-Freudians could hardly get published in the professional journals, much less the popular press. Hence Fresh died in obscurity, championing a paradigm whose time had not yet come.

The single variable of the Freshian paradigm was metabolic rate, but not metabolic rate as usually defined. To Fresh, a person's MQ, or "metabolizing quotient," was a measure not simply of gross calorie burn, but of the rate at which one "*produces* and *processes* all information, including, but certainly not limited to, oysters

Rockefeller." According to this curiously cybernetic definition, virtually all human activities, from arguing with one's spouse to watching a play, were "metabolized" at varying rates, and the texture of an individual personality was to a great extent created by "the interfusion of the production (or Output) rate with the processing (or Input) rate."

Production/Output meant basically one's rate of volubility, or reactivity to external stimuli; processing/Input meant one's "tolerance" for those same stimuli. Since one could be either "high" or "low" with regard to the Input and Output components, Fresh derived a four-category typology of human personality. He illustrated it in this distinctive box matrix:

OUTPUT

		High	Low
I			
N	*High*	HI-HO	HI-LO
P			
U			
T	*Low*	LI-HO	LI-LO

Fresh's most valuable contribution to personality theory, perhaps, was not this typology per se, or even the insights he afforded into famous personalities in history (Napoleon, for example as a classic HI-LO, and da Vinci as a LI-HO), but the application of the theory to personal affairs. Insisting that most marital mismatches could be prevented by a premarital "MQ screening," he established a London marriage-counseling service that succeeded, so he claimed, in reducing the city's divorce rate by eighteen percent over five years. In this pioneering work, only now being recognized, Fresh anticipated the breakthroughs of such modern giants as Wayne Dyer, Leo Buscaglia, and Dr. Ruth.

Irritated by neglect, Fresh became increasingly peevish and turned, in the 1920s, to parodies of his successful colleagues. His nose-thumbing analysis of Freud's friend Wilhelm Fliess, *The Nasal Stage* (1921), is a small gem of invective. The less accomplished slap at Sir Francis Galton, *Shoe Size as a Predictor of Genius* (1925), exposes the older man's birth-order theory as a classic case of the *post hoc ergo propter hoc* fallacy. His characterization of Jung, in a speech to the London Theosophical Society, as "P. T. Barnum masquerading as Rodin," remains the most acute dismissal of Swiss *fausse pensée*.

The Judas Factor *(1915)*

Clive Staples

To most academicians, popular historian Clive Staples has generally been considered a crackpot. Because he was distantly related to John Wilkes Booth (and made no attempt to hide it), his book on "the significance of treachery in human history" was seen as perverse special pleading, a stab at resuscitating the honor of his third cousin by painting his action as "historically necessary." Actually, there was more to *The Judas Factor* than that, as contemporary historians are coming to admit. The recent judgment of Rennart Ganelon, that the Staples thesis is "no less blinkered than that of Beard or Turner," is fast becoming accepted wisdom: witness the 1985 meeting of the Hispano-Nordic Oral History Society, whose theme was "Why We Need Our Villains."

Born in Missoula, Montana, Staples was educated as a straight-line fundamentalist—"nearly a Manichean," he later acknowledged—but under the influence of the Reverend William Bonney at Missoula State University, he was converted to Anglicanism, and it was a sophisticated, High Church view of causality that he brought to his study of human malice. "What I have done," he explained in his preface, "is to apply the doctrine of the Fortunate Fall to those of God's creatures who are clearly fallen—to test whether this Creation, or any Creation so conceived and so dedicated, could long endure without their baleful aid."

Arguing that "without Judas there is no crucifixion, and without crucifixion no redemption," Staples used the villain of his title as evidence that "evil leads to good"—but Judas was by no means the only example. In a quaint reversal of the *sic semper tyrannis* argument, Staples demonstrated that Brutus's murder of Julius Caesar paved the way for the fall, not the rise, of the pagan Roman Empire; that Benedict Arnold's treachery at West Point strengthened the American patriot cause; that Charlotte Corday's murder of Marat "saved" the French Revolution; and that his ancestor Booth's April madness made Reconstruction palatable to the South.

The Judas Factor appeared in the darkest days of World War I, and there is some reason to believe that the staunchly anglophiliac Staples meant it as a patriotic gesture. "Without the rash act of a wayward Serbian," he wrote consolingly, "the English-speaking peoples would not now be engaged in a conflict whose outcome will be the survival of democracy." To endorse this unique proposition, Staples went so far as to found a Gavrilo Princip Society, named after the assassin of Archduke Franz Ferdinand of Austria, and mounted a letter campaign to applaud the gunman for "pushing Progress forward." The appeal was tepidly received, and Staples disappeared from public view. He surfaced briefly a year later to protest the execution of Princip and then retired to a Delaware marigold nursery which he named, audaciously, Potter's Field.

High Jinks (1919)

Maximilian Vogelhund

Today the name Max Vogelhund is known only to those trivia buffs and pop-culture scholars who remember that his World War I nom de guerre Schnapsi inspired Charles Schultz's canine ace Snoopy or that his surname, which is the German equivalent of "Bird Dog," provided a title for the Everly Brothers' 1958 classic. Both connections are more than casual, because the flyer was certainly as self-inflated as Snoopy, and his sexual appetite was certainly voracious. But these details obscure his original importance as a jejune Rambo as well as his literary value as the author of the world's first "airborne memoir."

Born in Bavaria, Vogelhund emigrated to England in 1909 and fought throughout the Great War on his adopted country's side. A spirited account of his war experiences, *High Jinks* sold well throughout the 1920s, not only for the obvious nationalistic reasons, but also because of the book's lubriciousness and because the author claimed it had been composed, in toto, while he was in the air.

As to the lubriciousness, one may best get a flavor by citing chapter titles. An initial, lyrical description of the joys of flight is called simply "Getting Off." The chapter on his first kill is entitled "Scoring," and that on his second "Another Dirty Fokker Bites the Dust." The notorious chapter 7, where we meet his mysterious co-pilot "Miss Immelmann," Vogelhund calls "Why They Call It a Joystick." And chapter 19, where "by pushing all the right buttons" the pair shoot down four Germans in one morning, he entitles "We Invent the Immelmann Turn-On."

As attractive as such double entendres were to Vogelhund's Roaring Twenties audience, however, the real reason for the book's quick success was the author's claim that it had been composed largely during breaks between dogfights, as an instant recollection of moments of truth. "It was Emerson [sic] who said he could not live his life and write it, too. I have endeavored to transcend the transcendentalist by accomplishing both matters simultaneously." Thus the book achieved an immediacy that recommended it to a thrill-seeking generation. The sexual features of the narrative, of course, did nothing to lessen this appeal.

Sadly, Vogelhund did not live to see this. While on a "purely pleasurable" junket with Immelmann, he became (in her coy phrasing) "agitated by our cockpit activities" and died crashing his plane into a haystack. It was left to his companion, who survived the crash, to squire the book into a contract, and thus gain her lover a posthumous fame. She was also responsible for starting the rumor that since Vogelhund "came as he went," he was in a sense still alive. Among the spinoffs of this theory in the late 1920s were a spate of mediums who claimed that *High Jinks* literally "spoke" to them; and the common graffiti "Immelmann Turn On, Tune In, Drop Out" and "Bird Dog Lives."

Maybe the First Good Novel (1921)

Macedonio Fernández

Before García Márquez, there was Borges, and before Borges, there was Fernández. This completely forgotten Argentinian master of the *ficción* haunted the literary demimonde of Buenos Aires for a decade before meeting "the librarian poet" in 1929 and becoming, almost overnight, the lever that flipped Borges into narrative. Borges himself acknowledged the debt when he dubbed himself "Alejandro el Pequeño," merely coloring in the brilliant sketches of *"el grande Macedon."*

Fernández's imposing personality had something to do with his shock effect on the younger man, but what clinched the deal was this "novel not a novel" in sixty chapters—the first fifty-nine of which were couched as "essential prologues." The "Borgesian" themes here are many and blatant. The playful erudition, the centrality of dreams, most of all the aggressive implication that reality is what you say it is—these themes animate the book with febrile intensity, proving again and again Fernández's conviction that the business of fiction is not to mimic reality, but to "distract."

An implacable foe of realism, Fernández was especially hostile to those "pseudo-realists" (particularly Cucharra and Benevolencia-Guzmán) who "satisfy the reader's lust by giving him hallucinations, the show of forms that allow him to believe he is alive." "I want the reader to be aware, at every moment, that he is *reading words*, not witnessing a life. . . . I want to gain him as a character in his own story, so that he senses, if only for an instant, his evanescence."

To define a "plot" or a cast of "characters" for this collage of echoes would be a project about as sensible, to use Márquez's appreciation, as "to employ a calibrator to measure ice as it drowns your fingers." As the preponderance of "front matter" makes clear, the "design" of *La novela primera y quizá buena* is not dramatic or even narrational, but "alchemically boring"; the intention, like that of his most famous story, "The Squash That Became the Cosmos," is to allow facts to "flower into truths," so that by observing any single object, any single image, with complete attention, the reader may "instantly solve the enigma of the universe."

Whether or not this project is realized, of course, depends on the rigor and "negative capability" of each new reader. "I want only one," Fernández once told Borges, "for that is enough in the museum of eternity." Taking himself as that one potential "negative champion," Texas critic John Herndon once wrote what is perhaps the single best summation of Fernández's achievement. "Macedonio is one of those discoveries, like the Americas or Sutton Hoo, that revolutionize perspectives, pushing back cultural horizons like so many cardboard façades and confirming unexpressed suspicions that, after all, the conventional wisdom might be bunk."

The Found Poems (1926)

Rolly Keach

The austere genius Rolly Keach needs no introduction to serious students of modern poetry. Although he never attained the succès d'estime of Eliot and Pound, and has often been dismissed as atavistic in outlook, his crisp, somber lyrics speak to the human thirst for pensiveness with an incisiveness that transcends time and school and that has commanded respect among his most famous rivals. Eliot himself, it should be remembered, once shared a podium with the New Jersey poet, and Pound—no slouch at cogitation himself—called him "a fair hand with a line."

Given such praise, Keach's lifelong contention that he did not actually write his poems, but "picked them up here and there, I cannot really say where," resonates with disingenuousness. It is understandable that he attempted this coy dissimulation with regard to his early *Newspaper Worse*, for the book lived up to its name. But his later work—*The Penguin's Book of Quotations*, *Counterfeit Classics*, and most blatantly *The Found Poems*—are of such a consistently high quality that they make a mockery of his false modesty.

Take, for example, this brief excerpt from his scathing look at human conflict, "They Call It War":

> . . . *no arts, no letters, no society; and*
> *Which is worst of all, continual*
> *Fear, and danger of violent death, and the life*
> *Of man solitary,*
> *Poor, nasty, brutish, and*
> *Short.*

What vividness, what economy, what control over turgidly evanescent material! Can there be any doubt that such a poem is *innergefühlt?* Or consider the bleak lachrymosity of this exchange from Keach's much-quoted "Conception":

> *Pray, my dear, quoth my mother, have you*
> *Not forgot to wind up the clock?*
> > *Good God! cried*
> *My father—Did ever woman since the creation*
> *Of the world*
> > > *Interrupt*
> > *A man with such a silly*
> > > > *Question?*

Again, the characteristic control, coupled here with an exquisite, Poundian sense of wrenched design. The same sense glares haughtily from the page in Keach's most famous lyric, the brilliantly sparse "Consolation":

> *Ahm no gud*
> *At bean noble but*
> *It duznt take much to*
> *See that the prahlems of 3 lttl peepul*
> *Doan mount to a hill a beans in this crazy*
> > *Whirled.*

This poem, as is well known, marked the beginning of Keach's prolific Perth Amboy period, and it was also the "pivotal" piece (Number 53, as always) in the *Found Poems* collection. To those who know Keach's expertise only through this lyric, the remainder of the book cannot be too highly recommended.

One Swell Foop *(1927)*

William Archibald Spooner

The Reverend William Archibald Spooner taught for fifty years at New College, Oxford, where he astounded his associates with a capacity for ostensibly inadvertent humor. He once apologized to a visitor for not being able to present his wife—while the poor woman was standing beside him. To a dinner partner whose hand he had pierced with a fork, he replied dryly, "I believe that's my bread." And, in countless instances, he tortured the English language into mirthful lunacy by transposing the initial consonants of contiguous words; the resulting oddities—"well-boiled icicle" for "well-oiled bicycle," "our queer old dean" for "our dear old queen"—have since his tenure been called "Spoonerisms."

One Swell Foop is solid evidence that the man knew exactly what he was doing, and that his supposed malady—the technical term is "metathesis"—was the result of donnish cunning. The recently discovered New College manuscript has been ably edited by Beatrice Fetch, and in her introduction she portrays the Reverend Spooner as a subtle self-publicist, "using dottiness much as Einstein used ketchup on his tie—as a certification of his specialness."

Written in his last years at New College, the manuscript provides a fascinating glimpse of Oxbridge society in what Fetch calls "the days of wine and dahlias between the wars." The memoir is notable for acid portraits of university characters—Evelyn Waugh appears as "that disagreeable little man who could never keep his bottom buttoned"—and for a quirky but pellucid style. The *Literary Times* praised Spooner's rhythms as "the most luxuriantly periodic since Oscar Wilde's," and even Ricky Jay Boozer, editor of the shamelessly anglophobic *America First News*, says, "The guy was a real honker, for a Brit."

But the volume's principal charm is a double version of the

famous "mystery" lecture that Spooner is supposed to have castigated a lax student for "hissing." "Comparing the original and the 'metathetized' texts side by side," Fetch notes, "you see Spooner as a toffy Josh Billings. Out of a sensible but quite boring survey of Roman history, he has concocted a tapestry of timeless ringers. His self-imposed affliction was pure theater."

One need not be as adulatory as Fetch to admit that the doctored version of Spooner's text is an improvement over the original. His rendering of Caesar's dying words as "Hey, brew, tootie," his description of Nero "riddling while foam burned," and his image of the Vandals taking a "hedge slammer" to the Roman Forum—these are classic inversions that make the volume, in Fetch's summation, "one swell foop of a memoir."

What, Me Worry? (1928)

Alfred E. Neumann

As any reader of *Mad* magazine can tell you, Alfred E. Newman is the goofy-looking, trusting soul whose face adorns the cover of every issue, and whose befuddled fatalism has, since the rag's inception in the 1950s, always served as its guiding shadow. What few readers know—and what the management of that critical force in American popular culture has always denied—is that there was a real Alfred E. Newman, and that his autobiography *Ich Sollte Mich Sorgen?* (literally "I Should Worry?") gave the founders their loopy inspiration.

The original Newman (he spelled it Neumann) was an Austrian street sweeper turned financier who, in the great currency marathon of the Weimar era, danced in and out of fortune several times. In his recollection of his "tango with Dame Fickle," he stressed the role of chance and serendipity—a not surprising emphasis given the fact that he made his initial coup by sweeping up a worn pfennig that turned out to be worth a million marks. "I saved it," he confessed, "because I am fond of *Schmutzligchen* [little dirty things]; how could I know it once had been owned by J. S. Bach?"

In spite of its heavy reliance on Viennese street slang, Neumann's book was well known to English readers between the wars. It was translated first as *It Takes a Worried Man* (1928), then as *Nobody Knows the Tsuris I've Seen* (1933), and finally as *What, Me Worry?* (1938) before London censors, fearing the British public were beginning to see the Huns as too human, put Neumann officially on the Very Back List. Quite ironic, considering the author's lack of political sensibilities. Describing himself as a "devout coward," he disavowed affiliation with all parties and saw the nascent Nazi groupies as especially offensive: "The last time I was in Bavaria," he wrote, "they were still calling Adolf the Munich Putz."

Given the renown of the book in the 1930s, it is inconceivable that *Mad*'s editors had not heard its name. Their famous announcement, in the March 1959 issue of *Publishers Weekly*, that "the similarity of names is purely coincidental," was Olympian in its disingenuousness. One waits, still, for their confession.

Unknown as he may be in America, Neumann is famous in his native land for inventing two telling phrases. One, the Austrian pseudo-credo "Elsewhere things are serious but not desperate; in Austria they are desperate but not serious," he uses to describe a "gutter evening" when all he can find to eat are *Wienerschnepfels*—slang for both woodcock and streetwalker. The other is his assessment of "Herr Doktor Arzt Professor Traumdeuter Freud" (Mr. Dr. Dr. Prof. Dreamreader Freud) as *eine überbezahlte Sofakartoffel*, or "an overpaid couch potato."

The Kitchen Poet *(1931)*

Owen Llewellyn

Llewellyn, a professor of Welsh literature at the University of Aberystwyth, spent much of his academic career publishing studies of the medieval lyricists Owain Cyfeiliog and Daffyd ap Gwilym. In 1929, after the international stock-market crisis wiped out his modest savings, he abandoned his financially barren profession and attempted "to make a fortune by giving the dolts what they want." What the English reading public wanted was cookbooks—Emily Cosgrove's *101 Ways to Cook Bangers and Mash* had just entered its fourth printing—and so Llewellyn, marrying his literary expertise to market demand, prepared a selection of "Great Writers' Favorite Dishes" which he published as *The Kitchen Poet.*

The volume was presented with considerable fanfare—full-page ads in the *Literary Times*, for example—as a bona fide compendium of authors' recipes, but Llewellyn's puckish appearances on BBC radio as well as the occasional columns he wrote for *Punch* under the name "Poetaster" made it clear that the book was a spoof. Whether all readers got the joke is unclear; what is clear is that cuisine gave the professor a notoriety and an income that no amount of scholarship could have provided. He seemed quite content to have thus altered his perspective. "To those of my former colleagues who claim I have debased the dignity of the classics by this venture," he announced impishly to his radio audience, "I say that even Chaucer used his Pandarus, as a way of putting meat on the table."

Llewellyn's success owed less to the dishes themselves than to the way in which they parodied authors' styles. Indeed, as he acknowledged in a coy introduction, the collected recipes were, "in accordance with the well-known British apathy about matters gustatory, more a way to our poets' hearts than to their cupboards." Thus the author was relatively uninformative on precise measurement or seasoning, and contented himself with gourmet-style descriptions of such items as Daniel Defoe's cannibal stew and Charles Dickens's poorhouse gruel.

Stylistically, the descriptions fit their supposed authors. Here, for example, is Llewellyn as Alexander Pope, in a coupleted recipe for "Tory tart" that mocks the continental innovation of whitening, or "blanning," wholegrain flour:

> Yet shun the French king's fancy, presume not flour to blan;
> The proper grain for Englishmen is bran.

Here he is as Oscar Wilde, extolling the virtues of a dessert known as "Lady Windermere's flan":

> It is impossible in this recipe, as in life, to introduce too much honey. Mellifluity openly enchants but secretly frustrates. As frustration is the most exquisite of pleasures, it follows that no flan can be too sweet.

And here he is as Ernest Hemingway, that perennial favorite of parodists, whose book *The Sun Also Rises* was a best-seller in the late 1920s:

> To make a great hunter's stew you must be a great hunter, and there are not very many great hunters around and so there are not very many great hunter's stews. There are some good hunter's stews but there are many that are not so good because they are made by hunters who are not so good, and it is better not to eat these stews because they will bring you dishonor and a bellyache.

Clearly, Llewellyn's delight in this book was in assuming the voices of the Great Writers: the recipe format was a pretext for an eccentric survey of English literature.

At least one modern academic has found that pretext of pedagogical value. Alyce Wilderstein, chair of the English department at Hot Springs Regional University, requires the Llewellyn "spoof" as a supplementary text in the freshman survey course. "We find that students warm quicker to the classics when they are presented with a bit of fun. My best student in twenty years here is now a professor of Old English at Harvard. She tells me that what first enthralled her about Beowulf was Llewellyn's recipe for fricassee of monster haunch. And frankly all of our students would rather read Wordsworth's pan-fried trout recipe than his poems."

Surfing the Ogallala (1932)

Winston and Myra Jones

Jazz-age aficionado Redge Faraway says of the Joneses' memoir that it "makes Scott and Zelda's wild garden parties look like wild garden parties." Most readers of this Roaring Twenties picaresque have agreed, for in an era when more people went over Niagara Falls in a barrel than at any time before or since, the daredevils Winston and Myra set new standards for madcap inspiration—so much so that, as I have pointed out in my *Cat's Pajamas*, their exploits gave us "keeping up with the Joneses."

The Joneses, who began their professional careers as circus aerialists in Texas, first came to national prominence in 1925, when they challenged the aging Harry Houdini to "lock *them* up, then watch the fun." They gained considerable publicity from his refusal ("I don't play in the bush leagues," he explained), and went on to a series of exploits usually involving water or heights. Their memoir documents many of these adventures, including their handcuffed ascent of the Eiffel Tower, their daring jump *up* Niagara Falls, and of course their service as "debtor checkers" in the Crash of 1929, when they made a fortune in side bets by catching would-be suicides falling from buildings: "We were trapeze catchers back in the Texas days," they explained. "Learn to catch one body, you can catch them all."

But the most interesting aspect of the Joneses' book was the one that gave it a title. The Ogallala Aquifer is a huge body of water extending underground from Texas up to Canada, and from the Mississippi River to the Rockies: a subterranean vestige of the vast inland sea that covered North America in the Epicene. The Joneses' first major feat, after leaving the Texas high wires, was to tunnel into this reservoir around Cheyenne, Wyoming, and then ride its gentle slope eastward through Nebraska, Iowa, and Illinois before emerging from another tunnel outside of Chicago. They called this weeklong journey into darkness a "surfing adventure" rather than a boat ride because they traveled on a banana-shaped raft, "like the Mezkins use in the Gulf."

To the Joneses, this youthful escapade, even though it gained them only a local notoriety, remained a high point of their careers. "Not in all the marvels we have seen since—not the surging of slippery Niagara, nor the company of eagles during a wing walk—have we experienced the pure, quiet ecstasy that came as our lanterns sliced dimly on and we spied the endless reach of Earth's darkest ocean. Our seven days of uncertainty on the 'eighth sea' will always be the most thrilling in our memory."

Because of the danger of the undertaking, their feat did not produce many copycats, and none of those that did follow their lead ever made it all the way to Chicago. Feeling guilty about these few lost souls, the Joneses in 1927 formed the Ogallala Aquifer Rescue Society (OARS) to recover lost underground "surfers"; it failed within a year for lack of funding.

Their more public achievements soon overshadowed the aquifer ride, and the Joneses became, in the words of one historian, "a conventional phemonenon." They died, together, in 1931, of "antiquarian's emphysema" (bookworm lung) contracted during a stunt at the New York Public Library. Despite their reputation as mere twenties oddities, it's clear from their memoir that the surfing feat puts them in the first ranks of mystical explorers. "There are only two skippers I respect more than myself," William F. Buckley admitted recently. "Christopher Columbus and Win Jones."

Canary Row *(1933)*

Lester Stoed

An offbeat example of Depression protest literature, this "avian fable" described the giant Wragley coal mine in West Virginia from the perspective of an opinionated canary brought into the mine as a "gas alarm." Singularly displeased with the arrangement, the bird takes every chance for revenge, often with humorous results. The miners call their doomed pet Bertie, but it prefers to be known as the Yellow Peril, "because if I hold my breath long enough, these buggers will never know what hit 'em."

Actually, the practice of using birds as early-warning signals for poisonous gasses had pretty much expired by the 1930s—the Davy safety lamp served the purpose better—and it is a sign of Stoed's atavistic politics that he considered the image still apt. His resentment of "the bosses" knew no bounds, for he had been blacklisted and locked out in his youth, and he offered his novel as poetic revenge. But there was more heat than light in his attack: among the abuses he—or rather his feathered spokesman—blamed the mine owners for were the burning of the White House in 1812 and the extinction of the passenger pigeon.

Outdated as it may have been, *Canary Row* did express the "correct" sentiments for a 1930s proletarian novel, and was credited with considerable social influence. The Steinbeck connection is obvious enough, but the book has also been proposed as a possible influence on George Orwell's *Animal Farm*, which is quite ridiculous, and on his *Road to Wigan Pier*, which is not. It has also been suggested, by the Trotskyite Cartoonist Collective, that Stoed's hero was the prototype for Warner Brothers' Tweety Bird. Stoed's 1935 conversion to craft unionism dramatically changed his outlook. Embarrassed by the fable, he expatiated grandly in the socialist press about the need for higher wages rather than revolution. This led former colleagues to condemn him for backsliding—and for the Trades Union Congress to award him its Blood and Sweat Medal for 1936.

Stoed's vogue, like that of other "worker" writers, waned with the beginning of World War II, but he has enjoyed a revival in recent years, thanks to the Antivivisectionist League's adoption of suffocated Bertie as its 1981 Animal of the Year. This would have come as quite a shock to Stoed: he had the largest collection of stuffed birds in seven states.

Raymond Salaud (1949)

Lucien Choufleur

Raymond Salaud is one of those rare works of art—like Goethe's *Werther* or Mariachi's *Etudes Mexicaines*—that are more significant for what they generate than for what they are in themselves. This is an ironic thing to say about Choufleur, for he presented his novel as an *acte gratuit*, and would have been astonished to find that his influence, since his death in 1956, extended to such "contingent" arenas as popular movies and modern fashion.

A professional boxer up to 1946, Choufleur in that year discovered existentialism, and immersed himself in the writings of Sartre and Camus. Within a year he had become a café intellectual, building on the tradition of such *pugilistes cartesiennes* as Robert Cohen to ingratiate himself with the Deux Magots crowd and to earn a reputation (in the words of Gigi Sombreux) as "the only counterpuncher that Jean-Paul feared."

It was not enough. In the latter part of 1947, feeling still a "sometime member of the club," he began a work of fiction that would amalgamate the basic Left Bank theories with (in his ingenuous phrasing) "those images that have made me what I am." For Choufleur, this meant American *film noir*, subway billboards, and boxing newsreels. As a result, his need to impress the "big heads" battled constantly with naïve wonder at "low class" creativity, and the novel that he wrenched out of this tension offended Hollywood no less than his café patronizers.

Choufleur's character, Raymond Salaud, is a free-lance detective, very much in the Spade and Marlowe mold. But his impulse control is leaner than theirs; he justifies his frequent outbreaks of "gratuitous violence" by invoking Camus's Meursault as a patron saint, and by taking as his personal First Commandment the Dostoyevskian notion that "without God, all is permitted." Thus, when he suddenly punches a stranger in chapter 1—"blessing her with fortuity"—his justification is, first of all, Meursault, and then the honor that must be paid to one's own feelings. In his words, "It seemed like a good idea at the time."

The café crowd, recoiling at this "abuse" of the current cant, eased Choufleur out of the favored circles, and he ended up in Marseilles, boxing for brandy. But the reverberations of his work were widely felt. Mickey Spillane first, and then the *Dirty Harry* and *Death Wish* writing teams, acknowledged Choufleur as an influence on their dramatic styles, and Spillane has gone so far as to admit that "If that froggie hadn't whacked that little old lady, Mike Hammer mighta thought twice about plugging broads."

Choufleur's other claim to fame lies in the fashion field. Salaud's standard costume is not a trench coat but "black on black," and his female companion, the lustrous Cherche Femme, also dresses exclusively in "midnight magic." The vogue for "basic black" during the 1950s—in the haut monde as well as in the demi—has been traced distinctly to the Choufleur fad, and modern *bikers parisiens* also acknowledge his influence. No doubt this would have pleased the struggling author. His personal motto before 1950 was *Je suis moi* (I am me); after his shabby treatment by the Paris set, he changed it defiantly to "Paint it black."

The Digressions (1952)

Mimsy Borogrove

The reviews that greeted Mimsy Borogrove's one published novel were unanimous only in their extravagance. Admirers called the book an "instant classic," a "logophile's dream," a "glimpse of God's doodle pad," a work "that makes *Finnegans Wake* look like *Rebecca of Sunnybrook Farm*." Critics called it "grotesque," "inchoate," "gibberish." One said the author had "evidently transcribed the book from a nightmare brought on by pepperoni pizza"; another demanded she be hanged for verbosity.

The hyperbole of these reactions was understandable, for *The Digressions* was not so much a novel as a phenomenon. In the early 1950s, when Faulkner's recent Nobel Prize and the flap over the censorship of Joyce's *Ulysses* had made "stream of consciousness" a literary-party buzzword, it was generally assumed that those two writers had brought the technique as far as it could go. Borogrove, who then described herself as "a part-time logoclast, full-time dream merchant," consciously set out to prove this wrong by writing a 100,000-word novel in one sentence.

It is fruitless to define "theme" or "structure" for her book, because no two readers agree on what they are. One Borogrovian expert, Estuary College's Cavil Dunne, has suggested with epiphanous vapidity that "structure *is* theme." Mirabelle Newmark of the Gotham Grammar Collective feels that discussion of novel form is "passé—which is precisely why Borogrove is so important." And Colin Halley, author of *Why Critics Stink*, says that "the book, like a dream, is about everything, but especially about loss and Pareto optimality and tainted artichokes."

Whatever the book is "about," its texture is clearly unique. Consider a randomly chosen passage in which the author speaks of democracy, frozen dinners, and Tristram Shandy:

> ... *which in the course of human events not violated by the designs of lunchpail wizards, those gelid gourmandizers battening on to whatever crumbs of conscience (Shandy, don't make a gaffe, quoth* mi padre*) that cracker-barrel Jeffersonians and other cold-turkey farmers with their rabid gentility might pass on, if only for the fractured sake of* ...

One searches in vain here for the verb, and indeed the book has been described by one detractor as "an endless Germanic pseudo-sentence, the periodic form gone all wonky." Yet its divagating energy is clearly infectious: it has the unsullied charm of a fugitive perception transcribed without thinking onto paper. It was precisely this quality, not surprisingly, that made Borogrove a favorite with the Beat poets: Kerouac's estimation was "The chick's a gas."

Seldom read outside of academic circles since the 1950s, *The Digressions* is now enjoying a modest revival since its "discovery" by a West Coast "channeling" group. Spokes-entity Averill Bunch, known to his colleagues as Sham Seven, explains: "The Borogrove material is extra-planar, the author herself merely a mouth; locked in this text is Pure Mind, awaiting only the key of higher consciousness to be revealed." Asked to assess this latest reading of her book, Borogrove—now a parakeet breeder in Dubuque—commented cryptically, "Good, though."

Blanche *(1956)*

Van Than Xieu

The late 1950s in French culture marked the gradual fading of Sartrean influence and a rise in the power of the New Novel. Many Paris traditionalists felt that this innovation retarded rather than advanced the search for truth, but their uneasiness was trivial compared to negative reactions abroad. French colonials from Dakar to Dien Bien Phu revolted against the notion of a "depoliticized," experimental literature partly out of repugnance to the non-narrative, but more defiantly from the unavoidable recognition that the "silence" of Robbe-Grillet and his fellow *surfictionaires* muted the righteous outrage of their native lands.

This outrage evoked few literary classics, but it did lead to one *sur-sur-roman* that attempted to expose the inanities of Parisian hegemony by forcing experimentalism to an absurd conclusion. That "novel" was Van Than Xieu's *Blanche*: a book composed entirely of chapter titles followed by "veritably and irretrievably silent" chapter texts that, in the "resonance of muteness," both witnessed and undid Parisian style.

A few examples. In the opening chapter, cleverly entitled *"Première,"* the heroine Blanche, that "pristine avatar of the Caucasian fundament," speaks of an *ennui terminal*:

In the "glittering death" scene of the chapter *"Jusqu'au Point,"* where Blanche and her lover Maurice G. turn sensuality into its opposite and vice versa, we have this thinly remorseful coda to their pact:

And, in the bleak celebration that follows the victory at Dien Bien Phu, Blanche, once again abandoned to the vagaries of war, utters these careful words of condemnation under the brilliantly elusive title *"Après Diner"*:

*

---

* With typical acuity, Vinchon identifies this phrase as "the germ of the entire minimalist movement." See his definitive essay "Open Language" in Jerzy Wittle's collection *Deep Reading the Evanescent.*

In all these instances—and they scarcely suggest the book's variety—Blanche both espouses and undermines the cultural predilections of the intrusive French; when she finally leaves Vietnam, laughing at her would-be executioners, she infiltrates herself into our collective consciousness as (I am using Alsatian deconstructionist Frank Vinchon's terms) "the ultimate embodiment of policy gone amok." More than any of the French antiwar novels of the Algerian period, and more even than contemporary Buddhist feuilletons, this "empty drama" by one of Saigon's "forgotten scribblers" attests to the power of brittle laughter and of denial.

Miniplots *(1956)*

Clifford Notes

In 1955, as a graduate student in French literature at the University of Ohio, Notes—like many of his colleagues—discovered the usefulness of the multivolume *Masterplots* as an alternative to tedious reading. "The gist of *Candide* could be had there," he confessed once he had received his master's degree, "in the time it took to scan the Sunday comics. You could get Rousseau's *Confessions* in five minutes—just the space of a commercial break on 'I Love Lucy.' Even terminal bores like Proust were a snap: imagine copping *Swann's Way* in two pages."

But this "instant books" approach was only a beginning. Realizing cynically but realistically that, after graduation, most collegians forgot even plot summaries, Notes determined to go *Masterplots* one better, and to design a one-volume "condensation of condensations" for the use of "nonprofessional diggers in the field of learning—that is, poetasters, and belletristic name-droppers." The result was his instantly famous catalog of one-liners, that "indispensable guide to erudition in a nutshell," *Miniplots*.

The book's premise was set forth as a fanciful "syllogism." "One: All great ideas can be expressed in a single sentence. Two: No author, no matter how ingenious, has more than one great idea. Conclusion: Any book can be summarized in a single sentence." Notes set out to do exactly that. In a volume that was advertised as "no thicker than a billfold and only half as thick as my Uncle Harry," he distilled hundreds of world classics into sentences "that only an egghead could find lacking." A few examples will give the flavor of his gnostic dainties:

Beowulf: "Oafish Geat, after rubbing out monster and mom, gets zapped himself by fire-breathing dragon."

The Book of Job: "Neurotic deity proves he is top banana by totally destroying life of honest man."

The Song of Roland: "Frankish Custer commits suicide by refusing to blow his own horn."

Partly because of the coarse language, and partly because of what Notes called "the academic establishment's commitment to praising the emperor's new clothes," *Miniplots* has been widely denounced as a nail in the coffin of True Learning. At least one academic establishment, however, disagrees with the consensus. At the One-Minute University in New York City, all students are required to purchase *Miniplots* as "the fundamental text for all disciplines." University Chancellor Guido Sarducci, who ironically was Notes's adviser at Ohio, explains: "Studies have shown that five years after graduation, the average Harvard student has forgotten ninety-nine percent of what he has read. Here at the One-Minute University we are more efficient. We teach only the one percent that he remembers. And it's all here, neat and clean, in Clifford's guide. It is the microwave oven of higher learning."

A Prolegomena to Semiotics (1959-61)

Marilyn Monroe

During a press conference in the summer of 1959, Marilyn Monroe confessed that her dumb-blonde image notwithstanding, she was actually a "very dedicated reader." When asked to name a favorite author, she responded, immediately, "Lévi-Strauss." It was universally assumed she meant Levi Strauss, the blue-jeans manufacturer, but the *Prolegomena*, declassified only last year under the Freedom of Information Act, makes it clear that this contemptuous assumption was quite wrong. Not only was America's sex goddess well read; she was, in the words of Claude Lévi-Strauss himself, "one of only three people who understand me." (The other two were a Tiropia shaman and God.)

In the *Prolegomena*, after an incisive summary of Lévi-Strauss's major theses—that a "rage for order" typifies human consciousness, that symbols "signify" rather than "represent," that categorization generates comprehension, and so on—Monroe applies his typology to "that realm of human endeavor in which symbol and signification are most ineluctably intertwined": the world of representational art, and particularly film. Her theme is that "signifying" art always "bodies forth the contradictions of its social matrix," attempting through "rigid iconic artifice" to "expiate the demons of its own necessary irresolution."

Monroe's development of this thesis with regard to the "stable arts" from Caravaggio to Pollock is impressive enough, but when she enters her home turf, she becomes brilliant. Lucas Onderdagen, commenting on her chapter "Tainted Virgins: the Unabsolved Feminine from Bara to Lollobrigida and Back Again," writes that "her grasping of the *Kulturprinzip* was quite phenomenal." Structuralists on both sides of the Atlantic have agreed, and even "Perilous Paula" Cale, who has as little patience for abstruseness as any critic alive, has acknowledged that "Norma Jean was certainly onto something: this puts a whole new light on *Some Like It Hot*."

Suppressed first by Fox Studios (who feared the destruction of their star's carefully crafted image) and then by the CIA (who said it contained "sensitive" and "coded" material about John F. Kennedy), the *Prolegomena* manuscript lay in a Langley, Virginia, storage facility until 1984, when "aesthetician at large" Roger Frame finally secured its release. With Frame's fine editing and commentary, it was published on the twenty-fifth anniversary of Monroe's death and—in a final, posthumous irony—was immediately optioned by Fox. A critical edition, now in preparation, will include Onderdagen's "Monroevian thesis" dialogue with Roland Barthes, a deconstructionist "deep reading" by Paulo Savant, and a frame-over-frame fusion analysis of Monroe's films by the noted parase-miotician Josef E. Braun.

Salamanders Are People, Too (1965)

Josephine and Robert Calcott

The Friends of the Earthworm Society last year gave this slim, lyrical volume its highest honor: selection for inclusion on the Gold List of nature writings that have "significantly altered perceptions about our planet." It is difficult not to share this enthusiasm, for the Calcotts evinced a sensitivity to lesser species, not to mention an eloquence in panegyric, that would have shamed a Wordsworth or a Thoreau: it is not going too far to say, as one appreciative reader has said, that they "made John Muir look like a bounty hunter."

Ostensibly a "meditation on our amphibian friends," *Salamanders Are People, Too* has a broader scope than its title suggests. Like those of Renard or Moby Dick, the adventures of the Calcotts' slimy heroes generate musings on many wider topics, from the hazards of virgin birth to the Soybean Wars. The problems of the

main characters Sally and Newt, we are made to understand, are our problems, too: when this harmless pair is turned abruptly into road hash by the wheels of a speeding Coca-Cola truck, we sense, in the words of ecopundit Alice Nubbin, "the finger of doom flick our collective ear."

The means of their extinction was carefully chosen, for the Calcotts' benign obsession for many years was the amphibian rescue league Save Our Salamanders (SOS), based in isolated but *engagé* Granola Valley, an animal-activist haven in rural Massachusetts. SOS defended amphibian rights in many ways, but most visibly in an annual "Sally Walk" in which members escorted salamanders across highways so they might safely get to spawn. Thanks to the Calcotts' efforts, this odd little enterprise became a media event; local police were enlisted in the effort; and literally trillions of crawly things were saved from extinction.

In medieval folklore, salamanders possessed the ability to live in fire. Even though SOS and the Calcotts dismissed this belief as "charmingly noodle-brained," their detractors were quick to attribute it to them, and to suggest that the entire amphibian rescue effort masked an obscurantist—some said satanist—conspiracy. In 1976 a group called Save Our Species (the name was obviously chosen to confuse the public) mounted a vitriolic "Nuke the Newts" campaign that identified the Calcotts as "ooze-loving, devil-kissing species traitors" and included midnight ambushes on salamander nests. The group fell apart the following year, when its leader, Morris Bean, was jailed for "salamandalism."

Since 1970 the Calcotts have lived in Granola Valley, where they have helped to triple the salamander population, and where construction is being started on a marble statue that, in the words of sculptress Kiki Axolotl, will be "the largest stone newt in the Western world." Donations are being accepted; interested newt lovers may obtain the appropriate forms from SOS.

Constructs (1966)

Dieter Diddle

The concrete poetry movement of the 1950s and 1960s peaked with the sparsely expressive "construct" poems of the Dutch-born minimalist Dieter Diddle. So elegantly trim were his pictographic odes to building materials that Eugen Groningen, the leading German concretist, praised Diddle as "nonpareil among word-butchers: he makes my own work look baroque." Dot Matrix, the New York–based conceptual artist, agreed: in her estimation Diddle's poems "restored the dignity of the character qua character; they have earned for the designation 'literal' a newfound and long overdue respect."

As in all concrete poetry, the visual component of Diddle's work had much to do with its emotive power. Here, for example, is his notorious "Ode to a Cinder Block," which captures with beautiful economy the massive integrity of its subject:

```
XXXXXXXXXXXXXXXX
XXXXXX      XXXXXX
XXXXXX      XXXXXX
XXXXXXXXXXXXXXXX
```

Here, by contrast, is his deliciously sinuous "Slightly Flat Cable Spool," which overcame intensely heavy competition to win the Concrete Council's "Most Efficient Use of the Letter X" Award in 1965:

```
        XXXXXX
       XX      XX
      X          X
       XX      XX
        XXXXXX
```

Finally, Diddle's most daring exploration, the minimalist masterpiece "I-Beam Recumbent," in which (to augment Frank Lloyd Wright) typography *and* form follow function:

```
        II          II
        IIIIIIIIIIIIIIII
        II          II
```

These few examples should be enough to convince even the most hidebound traditionalist that Diddle has "out-Miesed van der Rohe," and that his "constructs" should take their place in modern poetry alongside such similarly innovative phenomena as Pound's *Cantos* and van der Rohe's own girder verse. If more evidence is sought, however, I can do no better than to quote a brilliant passage from Cicely Haddington's recent survey of "surpoetics," the highly acclaimed *Para-Meta-Mega-Language: Paladins on the Lexical Frontier*:

> *The narrational level in this poem has an ambiguous role: contiguous to the narrative situation, it gives on to the world in which the narrative is symbiotically undone (i.e., consumed) while, capping the preceding levels of discourse, it closes the narrative definitively, constitutes it baldly as utterance while it provides for and bears along its own ineradicable metalanguage.*

In response to this accolade, Diddle himself has responded: "I am utterly *#¢ by this reading; as the greatest of our Schrifters have always *gesagt*, it is truly ¢%*#@++! to be understood."

How to Think Good *(1968)*

F. W. Wiertz and Bubba Wilson

As the British philosopher and wit John Squire pointed out twenty years before this book's appearance in English, the "Wiertzian quest for certainty" was to the twentieth century what the Thomistic edifice had been to the thirteenth—"no less than a Herculean cleansing, by *force majeur*, of the Augean nastiness of the Western mind." It is a pity that Sir John never lived to see Wilson's emendations to his hero's classic, for the "Wilsonian" Wiertz is both more shocking and—in the best sense—more dilettantish than Wiertz qua Wiertz ever was.

Not that the German text was a minor achievement. Squire was quite right in proclaiming Wiertz "the first modern master of inconsistency," and in lauding his meticulous nonsystem of intuitive reasoning as "the best news for philosophy since sliced Broad." Indeed, the shock wave that Wiertz's *Prolegomena* sent through Europe in the years just following the First World War invited comparison with the still-smoldering Nietzschean craze: certainly Squire may be forgiven his slight exaggeration in calling Wiertz's "foggy mirror" metaphor "the most heuristic mental picture since Plato's cave."

But it was the Wilson translation—really a "transmutation plus potshots"—that turned the Saxon's magnum opus from "the Hope Diamond of the academies" into "everybody's rhinestone." One must not take the gemological comparison as derogatory. Wiertz himself had complained that his formula for Supraliminal Intuition had frightened many potential converts away,* and he prayed on his deathbed in 1940 that a "popularizer" would someday "do for my modest contribution what Mr. Spencer did for Mr. Darwin's."

That popularizer was found in Bubba Wilson, the "roughneck cogitater" who in 1965 was given a dog-eared copy of the *Prolegomena* by a fellow worker, and who, after reading three pages, decided to "give up oil rigs forever for a more dangerous game." "It was his chapter titles, I think, that turned me on," explained Wilson in 1969. "Down with Words; Down with Philosophers; Down with Systems—there was obviously a good mind at work here. And then his bursting of balloons, that was nice, too. Imagine calling Schopenhauer 'a dyspeptic mushroom on half pay,' or Zeno 'a lamppost without a lamp.' Priceless shit, if you ask me."

It was Wilson's genius to take Wiertz's ponderous brilliance and to present his concepts to the reading public in such a manner that "the dimmest bulb in Waco could understand it." When his version of the *Prolegomena* appeared in 1968 under the market-savvy title *How to Think Good*, it nudged Mortimer Adler off the best-seller list and created such an avid interest in philosophical matters that President Nixon was moved to ponder aloud whether "all this mumbo-jumbo might not be a commie trap."

Of the Wilson-Wiertz book's countless insights, one bears perhaps a special mention. Applying the Wiertzian formula to Wittgenstein's famous "picture theory," Wilson concludes with this gem: "Saint Ludwig made one big mistake. He interpreted natural phenomena as cosine functions! A clever pinhead could have seen the obvious: that an *object* must be intuited through its sine. Miss-

---

* Squire's well-known description of Wiertz's discovery bears repeating. "He had noticed, when weighing sections of an amoeba, that the weight of the sections was always less than that of the whole, and that the discrepancy varied with the temperature. For this Residuum, to which he chose to give the name Supraliminal Intuition, he discovered the formula: $\text{Cos } 65 \log 2 = 23 \sin 45 + \sqrt{2^{15}}$."

ing this, W. botched the entire algorithm, and with it (dare I say it?) the nature of reality." The ensuing firestorm of outrage from Wittgensteinians enlivened the 1969 social season. For the definitive account of that year's debate, see Alexander Sidarovitch's barbed memoir, *The Molehill Papers*.

The Mushroom Hunters (1971)

Lumpy Gravy

Written while Gravy (né Peter Schwartz) was studying mycology at the University of Texas, this skewed look at the passions of the 1960s tells the story of a band of "dedicated mind-benders," the Devotees of Psylocibin Experimentation (DOPE), who travel widely to find "the Ultimate Fungus." Gaia Czichtlo, quite sanely, has called it "the bastard child of Don Juan and Galadriel, midwifed by a whacked-out Euell Gibbons."

The legendary *hongo ultimo*, first described in an ancient Mexican codex, is supposed to bring enlightenment (what the Japanese call satori) to anyone who eats it—although at a considerable cost. In most cases, the codex makes clear, the "bliss state" is followed by the "stone state," in which the eater becomes catatonic and usually dies. It is a mark of the DOPE trekkers' spiritual courage, Gravy suggests, "that they are willing to risk their lives for the Big Lesson."

The novel opens in Mexico City, where the band convenes under the leadership of Mama Teonanacatl, a self-styled priestess of "vegetative inspiration" who divides her faithful into six cadres, one for each of the "great mushroom's" continents. The North American cadre is led by a "postmodern marimba genius" named Black Peter, and it is their quest that we follow throughout the book. It brings them from the peyote cults of the southwest to the "corned-beef hash" eaters of Iowa and Indiana, and finally to the subways of New York City, where a dream has told Peter the treasure lies.

The Ultimate Fungus, Peter believes, may be found "at the intersection of seven letters," and must be picked at the time of the gibbous moon, by a "hand that is not afraid to die." He solves the "fearless hand" issue elegantly, by giving each of his band a rabbit's foot with which to "pluck blessing from the earth when it appears." A problem he cannot get around so easily is determining the exact location of the prize. So many alphabet codes are used in the New York system that Peter's legions have a choice of thousands of intersections. Their frustration leads to bickering and occasional humor, as when band member Estes Kefauver complains to Peter, "I didn't sign on to swim in alphabet soup" and Peter replies, "Celery saves. Keep looking."

Although the DOPE members never do find the mushroom, their underground quest is seldom boring. Since fungus would obviously favor the dirt around the subway rails, they become adept at dodging trains and at "third-rail hopping"—a deadly game that Peter invents to stoke their courage. With their characteristic lime-and-lavender gimme caps (Mama Teonanacatl's sacred "colors"), they become well known to subway residents such as Boffy Bill, and get to exchange "trade secrets" regarding intoxicants. And throughout the novel, there are "daring escapes" from the dreaded Subterranean Pig Squad, who root for DOPE members no less assiduously than their four-legged cousins root for truffles.

The characterization of the subway police as swine and the "underground" locale of the story encouraged speculation about the book's political "message." Lumpy Gravy continually smirked at this, telling interviewers that his book was "just a gag." He has maintained this apolitical stance ever since. When Christopher Lemon-House asked him in 1988 which party he was supporting, his reply was, "There's only one party, man: BYOB."

Ayuh Speaks (1985)

Jimmie Ray Coles

For most of his adult life, Jimmie Ray Coles has been simply the town drunk of Gotchapatchouli, Louisiana. For an exhilarating seventeen months, however, he was the channel-cum-scribe to one Ayuh, a self-described "extraterrestrial misfit" intent on "reshuffling, and maybe stacking, the human deck." The "messages" that Coles claims to have received from Ayuh, transcribed verbatim in this volume, have fascinated New Agers and skeptics alike, for while "channeled" material is no longer unusual, Ayuh's pronouncements are more than usually peculiar. In the acute summation of entity-hag Laverne Shirley, "Ayuh is to the others as smoke to corn."

The most blatantly unique feature of the "Ayuh stuff," as Coles prefers to call it, is its multilinguality. About three quarters of the messages are in English, but even these are riddled with foreign terms, and the remaining quarter is a xenophobe's nightmare. Linguists have identified 97.3 known languages, in addition to lengthy passages of the mystifying Pschtt, which Ayuh describes as "our native tongue." No one has yet succeeded in deciphering this evidently synthetic language, and its unfathomability increases the book's appeal. (For a sample, see Appendix H.)

Ayuh's philosophy is also unconventional. While most channeled material is militantly bland—Shirley calls it "a fetid tapioca of secondhand Zen"—the Ayuh stuff is palpable, coarse, direct. Rather than the channelers' usual homocentric pantheism ("God is all of us"), Ayuh proclaims a simpler, earthier message: "God is a Jack Daniels with a beer chaser." Rather than the usual Blakean amorality ("There is no good and no evil"), Ayuh gives us commonsense verities: "Falling in love is good; falling down stairs ain't." And rather than proclaim the inevitability of cosmic evolution, Ayuh smirks: "You assholes are all on your own." No wonder that the Sausalito Trance Workers Union voted recently to boycott stores carrying the book, or that Marin County "metachanneler" Sheepa Zones has been fasting for a year and a half—taking only Ripple and Happy Meals—to "send this upstart Being back whence it came."

That Sheepa has not yet succeeded speaks, perhaps, to the strangest of Ayuh's oddities. Unlike other entities, he claims to come not from the past, or from a "higher" or "transpersonal" plane, but from a precise and quite mundane future. His home base is Jimmie Ray Coles's own Lost Cause Bar, and his time frame is 108 J.D.—108 years after Jack Daniels was declared a god, and 2222 in Earth time. He is throwing his barroom wisdoms back in time, he says, "so *homo arsholis* will know where he's heading: it just tickles me to see a puffer go bust."

The flurry surrounding this bizarre, entropic volume evidently has not fazed Coles himself. "On Ayuh's advice," he told me recently, "I'll be giving the money away to chili cook-offs." And he remains, with great dignity, the town drunk. "Fame I kin take or I kin leave. I been talking to spooks for twenty years. This is just the first what talked back."

Appendix A

Sautuola on the Altamira Spiral

The spiral of pebbles that Marcelino de Sautuola discovered in 1881 and identified as the oldest "book" in the world contained over fifty-seven varieties of etched glyphs. Working outward from a core of recurrent "heart" images, he was able to reconstruct the Magdalenian "vocabulary" and then the tragic tale told by the stones. This core contained the following dozen glyphs, given here with Sautuola's readings:

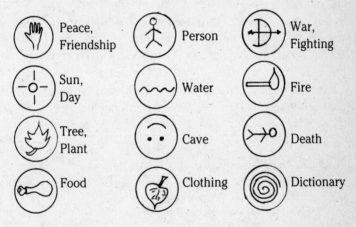

Sautuola was aided in his decoding process by the presence of two special markings. The first was a diagonal slash mark that transected some of the pictures and that he was able to interpret as "opposite" or "negation." Thus, while the glyph ⊕ meant "day" or "sun," the "canceled" ⊘ meant "night" or "darkness"; and the slashed version of the glyph for "clothing," ⊘ meant "lack of clothing" or "nudity." The second special marking was a crosshatched or "stitched" background, which seemed to indicate motion or action—in other words, what we would call "verbs." Thus ⊕ meant "to fight," and ◒ meant "to burn." This latter distinction, Sautuola later said, enabled him to "access Paleolithic grammar transformationally," and so "complete in one year the work of ten."

Appendix B

The Dudo Concordance

The themes of the twelfth-century poet Guillaume de Montmorcy-Burke are known to us only secondhand, through the line notation of Dudo of St. Quentin, unofficial scribe at the secluded Norman abbey. In this brief excerpt from the K section, we see not only the poet's metrical facility but also the satirical edge that might have encouraged his obscurity. The "swinish" knights were presumably sluggard nobles—those who enjoyed the privileges of their estate without performing its duties. The "cruddy Parson" of Lyric 24 is undoubtedly the ubiquitous Pastor Smudge.

Line	Lyric
A stranger Knight, that did his glory shew	3
An armed Knight upon a courser Strenge	7
To curry favor with the swinish Knights	11
That swinish Knight even among the reste	11
There lay the Knight all wallowed	11
Leadst you that swinish life, unworthy of a Knight	14
Twas to this verry Knght unseemely shame	14
Sent redness therof bye a different Knight	14
And knighthood fowle defaced by pricking swine	14
This gentle Knight himself so well behaved	15
Much was the Knight incensed with his lewd word	15
Thrice happie ladie and thrice happie Knight	15
They speyd a Knight fair pricking on the playne	17
I wot that was the Swinish Knight	17

Line	Lyric
The Knight that bore the swine's own quarters true	21
Yclept thou art not Knight but armored Swine	22
Strong Diamond, but not so stout a Knight	23
Thou cruddy Parson, whilom spake the Knight	24
To nightly steal and not so Knightly swoon	24
It was I wot a dark and stormy Knight	24

This excerpt is printed with the kind permission of Chaste and Buzzard, who publish the full concordance in two volumes.

Appendix C

The Bristoe Transcriptions

In his 1754 compilation of proverbs from the "great teacher" Griot Mbabo, Isaac Bristoe used a dual-entry transcription system to record first "the sound of the natives' feeble attempts to express themselves adequately in our manner" and second "the proper equivalent in the king's tongue." Given here are several examples from his book *The Wit and Wisdom of the Negroe*, reissued in 1968 as *Proverbs of Africa*. In each case the first spelling is the "feeble attempt," which linguists today call a pidgin (and which clearly is anything but feeble); the second is Bristoe's "king's English"; the third is a modern equivalent as given by *Proverbs* editor Hilla Agbodeka.

> *Bon mi, a fiva yu.*
> Born me, I favor (look like) you.
> (Children take after their parents.)

> *Yu tink sei na kapenta klin me?*
> You think a carpenter cleaned me?
> (Do you think I'm stupid, made of wood?)

Kopa di tok.
Copper talks.
(Money talks.)

Man get akis, wata fiva stik.
When a man has an ax, water looks like a stick.
(To a man with an ax, everything looks like a tree.)

Aion no fit hot if you no putam fo faia.
The iron won't get hot if you don't put it in the fire.
(Nothing ventured, nothing gained.)

Monki tok sei babu wowo.
The monkey says the baboon is ugly.
(The pot calls the kettle black.)

Man no fit dans i laf drom.
The man who can't dance blames the drum.
(The grapes you can't get are always sour.)

Troki wan fait bot i sabi sei i han shot.
The tortoise wants to fight but knows his hand is short.
(Your arm's too short to box with God.)

Appendix D

Ben Jonson's Pocahontas Poem

Of the English gentry who lionized Pocahontas during her time in London, Ben Jonson seems uniquely to have recognized that the adulation of the "dusky Princesse" was often demeaning. In his posthumous commendation "For the Lady Rebecca," he snipes at two enemies at once. One is rival poet George Withers, whose 1615 lyric "Shall I, Wasting in Despair" would earn him a niche in literary history. The other was the unidentified broadside writer, blunter than most in his racism, who called Mrs. Rolfe "but one more Nubian, with feathers."

The Withers poem and Jonson's reply first appeared together three years after Pocahontas's death, in *A Booke Called a Discourse of Love.* This was Withers's famous octet:

> Shall I, wasting in despair,
> Die because a woman's fair?
> Or my cheeks make pale with care
> Because another's Rosie are?
> Be she fairer than the day
> Or the flowry Meades in May,
> If she be not so to me,
> What care I how fair she be?

And this was Jonson's reply:

> Shall I mine affections slacke
> Cause I see a woman's blacke,
> Or my selfe with care cast downe
> Cause I see a woman browne?
> Be she blacker than the night
> Or the blackest Jet in sight,
> If she be not so to me,
> What care I how blacke she be?

The texts here are from the standard Jonson canon, edited by Herford and Simpson. They suggest that the parody is "too playful and kindly" to have come from Jonson's pen—a comment that vowel weighting alone reveals as sardonic.

Appendix E

Ukoan's White Belt: *the Okinawan Proof*

Aside from its literary merit, Ukoan's seventeenth-century martial arts classic is historically valuable because it demonstrates, *auctoritate cum incunabulorum*, that karate began in the Japanese-occupied Ryukyu Islands and not, as is commonly supposed, on Honshu. The relevant text is from Uku's second book, in the section entitled "A Famous Lie":

＊どういう人びとが空手を発達させたか？

ブルース・リーとデイビッド・カラディーンのおかげで、東洋的武術はすべて中国が発祥地であると考えられるようになった。同様に大した根拠もなしに、カン・フーという中国拳が、有史以前からある武術の中国起源の元祖であり、空手はその日本版であると言う人びともいる。今世紀初頭に西洋に空手を流行させた功績が日本にあるのは事実である。また「武器をもたない手」を意味する「カラテ」という用語自体も日本語である。しかし空手という武術形式は、日本人と

戦う手段として沖縄で始まったものである。

これは琉球諸島最大の島である沖縄が、日本の支配下で苦しんでいた十五、六世紀頃の話である。民衆の反乱を恐れた領主たちは、沖縄人に武器の所持を禁止した。そこで民衆は秘密の小集団を組織して素手・素足による武器なしの武芸を完成させた。彼らが練習した体の動きは、当時中国から伝来したばかりの少林寺拳法を改良したものだった。伝説によるとこの技はまた、インド人の僧ボディダーマの手で十六世紀に中国に伝えられたものであった。空手が一般に知られる武術となったのは比較的最近のことである。第一次世界大戦後まもなく、沖縄手と呼ばれる沖縄の技が、後に全日本空手道連盟長となった船越義珍師によって東京で披露された。これらの技は日本からアジア諸地域に、そして最後に西洋にまで広まった。

The attentive reader will observe that Uku uses a unique fusion of Hiragana and Katakana characters. His facility in this is the more remarkable because the latter were not invented until two hundred years after his death.

Appendix F

Bridget Colley on Gulliver's Travels

The editing that Jonathan Swift's housekeeper Bridget Colley performed on his manuscript of *Gulliver's Travels* made the book, in some ways, as much hers as his; it certainly cleaned out his verbal baggage. One example from Voyage I will make the point. Swift is describing the origins of the Lilliputian controversy between Big-Endians and Little-Endians—his code names for Catholics and Protestants. Colley's emendations and marginalia are in longhand.

... It is allowed on all hands, that the ~~earliest and most~~ primitive way of ~~fracturing~~ *breaking* eggs before ~~they are consumed~~ *we eat them*, was upon [*Avoid the passive tense*] the ~~more globular~~ *larger* end: but his present Majesty's grandfather, ~~in~~ [*Cliché!*] ~~the halcyon days of his childhood~~ *while he was a boy*, going to eat an egg, and ~~penetrating its fragile carapace~~ *breaking it* according to the ~~accepted~~ ancient practise, happened to cut one of his ~~digital appendages~~ *fingers*. [*Really, Sir!*] Whereupon the Emperor his father published an ~~imperial~~ edict, commanding all his subjects, upon ~~the gravest of~~ *great* penalties, to break the ~~comparatively pointed~~ *smaller* end of their eggs.

The complete Swift/Colley manuscript is now in Trinity College Library, Dublin. A fascimile edition is being prepared under the supervision of Swift scholar Gavin Grimes.

Appendix G

The Fleuve Family Tree

Readers of Marianne and Thérèse Colombard's intricate mega-novel began to complain after Volume 5 that they were having difficulty keeping the characters straight. To oblige them, the sisters included in Volumes 6 and 7 the following family tree, reproduced here courtesy of the original publishers, Guimard and Titreault. The identification *"personnages principaux"* was an understatement: the chart included less than a fifth of the novels' dramatis personae. Numerals in the left margin refer to the volumes listed below.

Volume 1. *Attention les doigts* (1824)
Volume 2. *Casser les vitres* (1826)
Volume 3. *En l'Oreille d'un mouche* (1827)
Volume 4. *Les Chasseurs du microscope* (1830)
Volume 5. *L'Arc en ciel enfumé* (1830)
Volume 6. *Au Revoir, Clermont-Ferrand* (1832)
Volume 7. *Attention les sous* (1835)

LA FAMILLE FLEUVE
(*personnages principaux*)

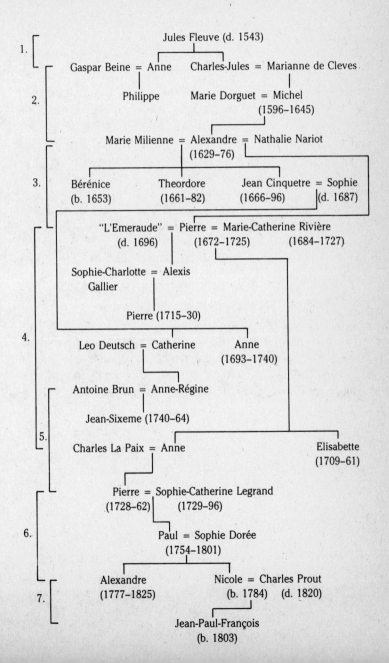

1. Jules Fleuve (d. 1543)

2. Gaspar Beine = Anne   Charles-Jules = Marianne de Cleves

    Philippe   Marie Dorguet = Michel
    (1596–1645)

3. Marie Milienne = Alexandre = Nathalie Nariot
    (1629–76)

    Bérénice   Theordore   Jean Cinquetre = Sophie
    (b. 1653)   (1661–82)   (1666–96)   (d. 1687)

4. "L'Emeraude" = Pierre = Marie-Catherine Rivière
    (d. 1696)   (1672–1725)   (1684–1727)

    Sophie-Charlotte = Alexis
    Gallier

    Pierre (1715–30)

    Leo Deutsch = Catherine   Anne
    (1693–1740)

5. Antoine Brun = Anne-Régine

    Jean-Sixeme (1740–64)

    Charles La Paix = Anne   Elisabette
    (1709–61)

6. Pierre = Sophie-Catherine Legrand
    (1728–62)   (1729–96)

    Paul = Sophie Dorée
    (1754–1801)

7. Alexandre   Nicole = Charles Prout
    (1777–1825)   (b. 1784)   (d. 1820)

    Jean-Paul-François
    (b. 1803)

Appendix H

Pschtt: the Ayuhan Language

Of the 97.3 languages that appear in Jimmie Ray Coles's 1985 transcription of Ayuh's "message to *homo arsholis*," all but one have been identified. The holdout is the vowel-poor confection that Ayuh calls "our native tongue," Pschtt. Here is a representative passage:

```
vcr bdr bvd fmb hqs gnp        hrh gpm vtl
vtl tsp zpg vrm sdi pkg mss nfl nwt pdt
hrh      ltd rps phd sba sob qtd lmn pqr
lcd lcd vcr kgb        hmc ghq frs dnb fob
sob tlc lst asf ama ftd g-d        bbl pct
rpm vtr vcr vct ncb kjv jcs dmz cbc tpk
tpk sbn dfc      sob std tko        lsm ftb
nwt pkg smv str uhf yds       g-d dam sfx
```

This mélange of noneuphonious consonants has been subjected to every code known to cryptography, but so far without avail. The $5000 prize being offered to a successful translator by the National Academy of Comparative Morphology remains, as of this writing, unclaimed.

For Further Reading

A major problem in researching neglected authors is that they have been neglected not only by scholars, but also by those assiduous encyclopedists from whom one might have expected greater diligence. A few exceptions have provided much of the grist for this mill. I am happy here to acknowledge their assistance:

John Abacus Anson. *An Encyclopedia of Middle Names* (1956).
A meticulously comprehensive index of famous people, arranged alphabetically by their middle names.

Aldo Cipolini. *Pharmacopeia Historica et Biographica* (1907–10).
The chemical addictions and dependencies of writers, artists, and historical figures. Cross-referenced by occupation, century, and chemical formula.

B. Reggie Coax. *The Frog Chorus* (1894).
The "amphibian impulse" in Western literature, from Aristophanes to Stephen Razin.

Abba Duse. *A Brief History of Stupidity* (1973).
The definitive abridgement of a classic survey. The chapter on "Phudniks from Socrates to Wiertz" is particularly entertaining.

Mary Whales, Lady Farquahar-Cholmesedly. *The Skeptic's Bible* (1879).
The major proofs against the existence of God, with detailed biographies of their heretical authors.

Stephen Gerain, ed. *A Checklist of Fugitive Manuscripts* (1928).
   The definitive catalog of writings mentioned in the literature
   but never located. Compiled by the Sorbonne's Chief of An-
   tiquities.

Maurice B. Morris. *The Pedant's Bible* (1945).
   One-liners for every occasion, with a major emphasis on Su-
   merian and Akkadian poets.

Jennie Niveau. *How to Smell a Sonnet* (1987).
   The most recent volume in the successful "Culture for Dopes"
   series, which also includes *How to Hyperventilate an Opera*
   and *How to Sabotage Ballet*.

Omar the Scribe. *Biblioteca Alexandria* (367; repr. 1833).
   A catalog of the Alexandria Library's burned or lost holdings.
   Titles only.

Nelson Quetch. *Twenty Lousy Ideas* (1961).
   The top twenty bonehead schemes in artistic and literary history, by a self-proclaimed "chaotophile."

Renfrew Stowe. *A Guide to Servile Thinking* (1878).
   The slave influence from Epictetus to Uncle Tom, breezily
   presented by Harriet Beecher Stowe's second cousin.

Q. P. Satchidanandananda. *Helpmeets and Also-Rans* (1981).
   The role of minor characters in world literature, from Sancho
   Panza to Portnoy's father.

Benjamin Trovato. *The Lesser Tradition* (1938).
   The Cambridge don's acerbic answer to the "tyranny of the
   Leavis crowd."

Atalanta Unger. *Plato the Charioteer* (1976).
   A guide to the athletic passions of literary greats, including the prizewinning essay "Dante Invents Bocce Ball."

Bovril Zut-Alors. *A Garland of Newspaper Verse* (1890).
   The "worst sprung-rhythm masterpieces from two centuries." With a special section on kittens.

Index of Authors

Index of Titles

About the Author

Born in New Jersey in 1944, Tad Tuleja is a graduate of Yale, Cornell, and the University of Sussex. He has been a journalist, editor, and researcher, as well as the author (or co-author) of twenty-five books. His short-entry reference books include works on word lore, popular beliefs, and social customs. Tuleja lives with his wife and three children in Belchertown, Massachusetts, and teaches at the University of Massachusetts in Amherst.